A BARTHOLOMEW MAP & GUIDE

WALK LOCH NESS & THE RIVER SPEY

INCLUDING INVERNESS & THE BLACK ISLE

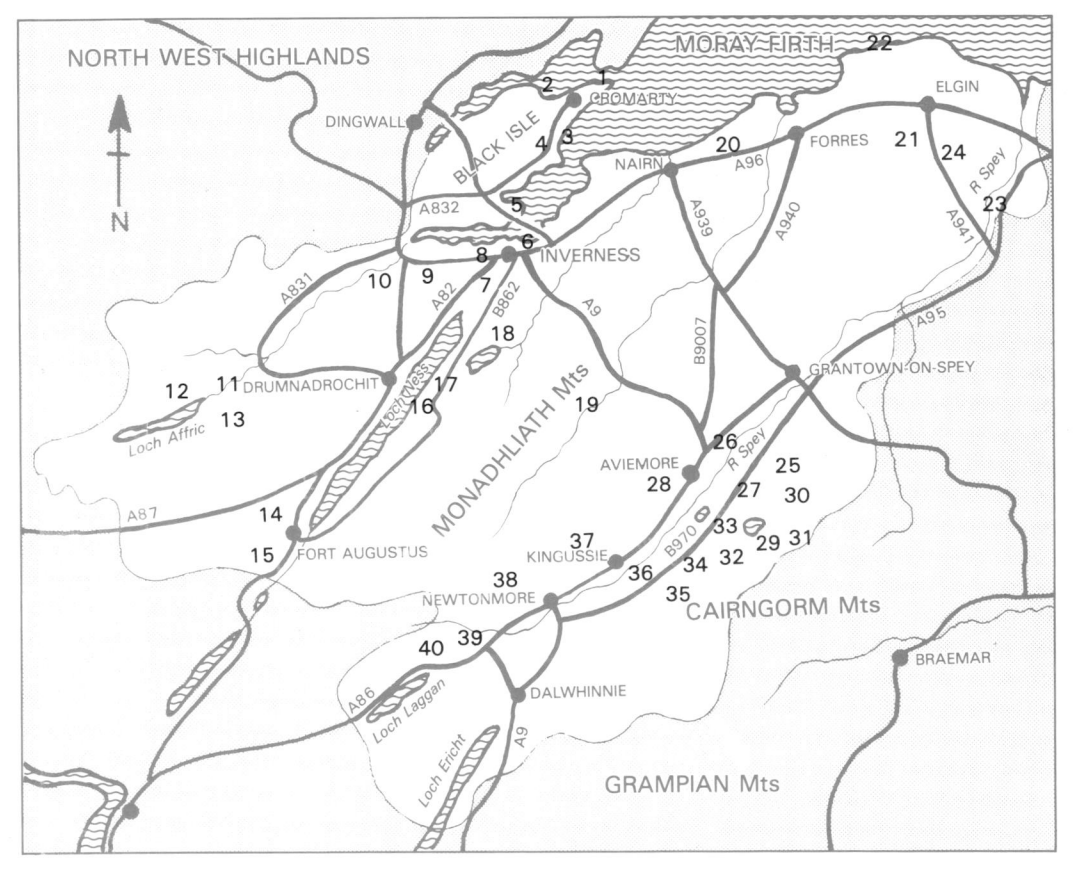

40 WALKS SELECTED & DESCRIBED BY RICHARD HALLEWELL
ILLUSTRATIONS BY REBECCA JOHNSTONE

JOHN BARTHOLOMEW & SON LTD EDINBURGH

British Library Cataloguing in Publication Data

Hallewell, Richard
    Walk Loch Ness and the River Spey : including
    Inverness and the Black Isle : forty walks.
    — (A Bartholomew Map and Guide)
    1. Walking — Scotland — Inverness (Highland
    Region) — Guide book 2. Inverness (Highland
    Region, Scotland) — Description — Guide book
    1. Title
    914.11'75'04858   DA890.I6
    ISBN 0-7028-0787-7

Published and Printed in Scotland
by John Bartholomew & Son Ltd,
Duncan Street, Edinburgh EH9 1TA

Copyright © John Bartholomew & Son Ltd, 1987

First edition 1987
Reprinted 1988

ISBN 0 7028 0787 7

The physical landscape of Britain is changing all the time
e.g. as new tracks are made, hedges grubbed up and fields
amalgamated. While every care has been taken in the
preparation of this guide, John Bartholomew & Son Ltd, will
not be responsible for any loss, damage or inconvenience
caused by inaccuracies.

About this book

This is a book of walks, all of which can be completed within a day. They vary in difficulty from gentle strolls to strenuous hill climbs, and are graded accordingly. Wherever specialist hill walking equipment is required it is specified. Each route is described, with information on the character and conditions of the route, and with a brief description of the major points of interest along the way. In addition there is a map of the route to aid navigation. Car parks, where available, are indicated on the route maps. The availability of public conveniences and public transport on particular routes is listed on the contents page and at the head of each route. The suitability of the route for dogs is also shown on the contents page. The location of each route within the area is shown on the area map inside the cover of the book. In addition, a brief description of how to reach the walk from the nearest town is provided at the start of each walk. For some of the walks, where there is a view of particular interest, there is an annotated illustration of the view. The following introduction gives a brief summary of the geology, history and natural history of the area, with reference to particular routes. Hopefully this will enable you to enjoy a greater appreciation of the area.

This is by no means an exhaustive list of the walks in this area, but I hope you will find it an interesting and representative selection.

Key

●●●	Route	⚞ ⚞	Marshland
══	Metalled Road	⋯⋯	Moorland
╉╉╉	Railway	⚘⚘	Coniferous Woodland
Ⓟ	Parking	♠♠	Broad-leaved Woodland
⸿	Information Centre	☁	Contour: shaded area
▵	Viewpoint		is above height indicated

INTRODUCTION

A Geology

The variety of the area's landscape, flora and fauna is a product of its curious, irregular shape, caused by a violent geological history. A mountain is a metaphor for stability, yet it is formed by its own mutability and weakness — the Cairngorms *(31),* for instance, are made of granite — one of the hardest of rocks — yet once they boiled beneath the Earth's crust, finally bursting through the surface and solidifying. They were then carved by the glaciers of the ice age; scraped into the rounded mass they form today. The rocks are not unchanging, they are susceptible to heat and cold and are constantly being altered: sometimes quickly, by volcano and earthquake; sometimes slowly — as today — by rainwater, wind and frost.

The features most easily observed from the routes in this book are those which were formed during the ice age. At its peak, the glaciers covered this entire area, with the exception of a few nunataks — mountain peaks which thrust up above the general level of the ice. The ice moved independently of the area's topographic features, pushed by the great ice sheets of the continent which reached across the North Sea. The ice broke segments of rock from the mountains as it passed; lifted them and, later, as it melted, deposited them. This accounts for the great variety of rock types found on sea shores and river beds throughout the area — some of them carried from what is now the European mainland — and for the 'erratics' — large rocks, dropped in unlikely positions, on hilltops or in the middle of wide plains.

As the glaciers melted they became smaller and retreated into the higher hills, where the air was cold enough and precipitation high enough to maintain them. Even today, in the cooler north facing corries of the high hills *(31),* drifts of snow linger well into the summer. If the weather were to become sufficiently cold, over a period of time, these would be the first areas to develop new glaciers.

The glaciers, although reduced in size, continued to move down the valleys: generating ice in the high corries (bowl shaped depressions in the hillside — common throughout the area) and slowly 'flowing' downhill, until the air temperature was high enough to melt the ice. Several obvious features in the landscape were caused by the ice during this period.

The progress of the glaciers gave the valleys a broad, U-shaped cross-section — very pronounced in glens such as Feshie and Tromie *(34,35,36)* — and left them so enlarged that they are now out of all proportion to the small burns and rivers which meander along their floors. In addition, the valleys of tributary streams, which were less deeply cut by the ice, were left 'hanging' above the level of the main valley floor. The valley floors themselves became filled with the matter scraped from the rocks by the ice — a mixture of fine gravel and small stones — either carried out by the streams of meltwater from the retreating glacier in a deep, even, fluvio-glacial deposit, or left in ridges of hummocky moraine. This gravel is quarried by man, and also by the elements: gradually being eroded by the valley stream and carried down to the river mouth. Along the coast of the Moray Firth this gravel has been swept ashore again by the prevailing tidal streams and blown inland, creating areas of unstable dunes — notably the Culbin and Findhorn sands, to the west and east of the mouth of the River Findhorn *(22)* which, in the past, proved volatile enough to bury whole villages and estates, but which are now stabilised by the planting of trees and marram grass.

The deepest cuts made by the glaciers were along fault lines, where two plates of the Earth's crust meet, and where the rocks are already crushed and weakened. The major fault in the area is along the Great Glen, and it is no coincidence that here the ice excavated Scotland's deepest loch: Loch Ness *(15,16),* over 800ft (250m) deep in places. Other lochs in the area formed by glacial erosion include Loch

Laggan, Loch Ericht and Loch Affric *(12)*. These lochs are long and thin; the smaller, rounder lochs are generally 'kettle holes': pools of water formed where lumps of ice had become embedded in the ground and then, after the main glaciers had retreated, slowly melted. Examples of these lochs are Loch Morlich *(29,32)*, Loch an Eilein *(33)* and Loch Garten *(25)*.

Most of the rocks in the Scottish Highlands are free of fossils, but the old red sandstone around the Moray Firth, formed by sediment accumulated on ancient lake bottoms, contains a number of fish fossils. This is the rock which gives the peculiar red tinge to the cliffs at Rosemarkie *(3)*, and which was studied by the local geologist and writer, Hugh Miller (1802-56) who was born and worked as a stone-mason, on the Black Isle. The cottage in Cromarty where he was born and worked is now a museum *(1)*.

B History

The land that the glaciers left was an empty one; only gradually becoming warmer, and only slowly being colonised by plant and animal life. The first Scots pine appeared around 8000 years ago, and the first settlers about the same time. Initially, the pines were the more successful, and the Highland regions became clothed in forests. Up to 3000ft (900m) above sea level the pines grew thickly, while the valley floors were full of broad-leaved woodland. A squirrel could have hopped from Moray to Galloway without once having to touch the ground.

For thousands of years the few inhabitants of the north lived a nomadic life; wandering through the forests, using only stone tools; as often prey to the hostile environment as predator on its plentiful wildlife. In time, a measure of agriculture became common, and the people began congregating in small settlements and evolving complex burial rituals at set sites — notably, in this area, at Clava, near Inverness.

Around 2500 BC the first few Celts arrived; followed, around 600 BC, by more warlike groups of the same people, with a knowledge of working iron. In later years 'Celtic' came to be associated almost solely with those people living on the periphery of Europe — Brittany, Cornwall, Wales, Ireland and north-west Scotland — but these were only the last strongholds of an extensive race who, at one time, inhabited the bulk of central Europe.

The descriptions of these European Celts, in the work of writers of the time, are illuminating. They portray an open, honest people, with a scorn for subterfuge or ploy, but disposed towards boastfulness and exaggeration; with a great sensitivity to insults, and a tendency to be short-tempered and violent; a lively people with a preference for bright colours, who built no cities, but lived in small villages ruled by local chiefs. This description could have been as easily applied to the Highlanders of the 18th century as to the Celts of the classical authors. Even their mode of battle had not altered; the headlong heedless charge of the clans at Culloden (1746) was precisely that observed by the Roman chroniclers.

One aspect in which the Highlanders did not match their ancestors was in their natural colouring. The European Celts were fair-haired but, despite a later infusion of blood from the similarly blonde Vikings, fair hair is comparatively rare in the modern Highlanders; proof that the earlier residents were not eliminated by the incomers, but integrated.

The Celts continued to arrive — not in concentrated 'attacks', but in small groups — throughout the next few centuries, bringing with them the various Celtic languages — forerunners of modern Scottish Gaelic, Irish Gaelic, Welsh, Cornish and Manx. They also brought, with their clannishness and warlike

disposition, the need for greater defence. They built large forts on easily defended hilltops. Examples of these forts are at Dun da Lamh *(39)*, in a splendid position above the Spey Valley; Farigaig, overlooking Loch Ness; Ord Hill, in the Black Isle; and Craig Phadrig *(8)*, in Inverness. A peculiarity of some of these forts is that their stone work has been fused under intense heat, caused by the ignition of the original wooden framework of the structure. Whether this ignition was accidental, or was intended to strengthen the walls, is a matter of conjecture.

As will be appreciated from the above, Highland history is less an exact study of listed facts, and more an exercise in the imagination. The subject has always contained a surfeit of speculation and a dearth of certainty, and such facts as there are, when they occasionally emerge, can usually stand at least a dozen interpretations, and tend to encourage dispute rather than dispel it. The very first recorded facts in Scottish history, from AD 84, are a perfect example.

The Romans had arrived in Britain in AD 78, and had found the islands a patchwork of separate, if broadly related, Celtic tribes. They had quickly subjugated the south, and then moved north, under Agricola, to complete their conquest. Not for the last time, the high hills and narrow passes were to prove a taxing obstacle for an invading army; one, indeed, which the Romans seem to have lacked the energy or inclination, or perhaps the ability, to overcome. The Roman Army marched up the east coast and, somewhere on the eastern fringe of the Grampians, between the River Tay and Inverness, fought a battle against the combined forces of the northern hill tribes. The tribes were led by a man called by the Romans 'Calgacus' — the Swordsman; the earliest recorded name of any Scotsman to have lasted to the present day. His army (of 30,000 men, according to the Roman historian Tacitus) was defeated, and he himself was killed, but the matter is shrouded in the gloom of history.

At any rate, the Roman army immediately withdrew, and made no further, serious, attempts to conquer the Highlands, preferring the expensive and inefficient alternative of building defensive walls across the breadth of the country (Hadrian's Wall in AD 122; the Antonine Wall in AD 143), thus allowing the northern tribes free space in which to organise their numerous, and often successful, attacks against their new, unwelcome, neighbours.

The site of Agricola's battle may well be within this area, but no one has been able to identify it with any certainty. The Romans called it 'Mons Graupius'; referring to the northern tribes as 'Picts', and to the largest tribe of the area as the 'Caledonians'.

Hadrian's Wall was finally overrun in AD 383, and the Romans departed soon after, leaving the north still free, and as impenetrable to the historian as it had been before they arrived.

The difficulty is partly one of language, for, as different as Welsh is from Gaelic, so was the language of the Picts from either. It was a distinct strain of Celtic, intermingled with the language of the pre-Celtic, bronze age Highlanders, and, although it was in use at least until the 10th century, and probably longer, not a single complete sentence of the language has survived, and nothing which can be translated with certainty.

The Pictish kingdom was a large and a powerful one, covering most of the Highlands and all of the area covered in this book — Inverness was a local capital — yet little remains as proof of the extent of their rule except a few place names and a collection of carved stones. These beautiful monuments are evidence of a distinctive and sophisticated national style, but they are cyphers, as obscure as their makers. They were produced between the 6th and the 9th centuries — a series of slabs, decorated with intermingled images; representational and abstract — and vary in content; pagan, Christian and secular.

In this area the best examples are the

Rodney Stone at Brodie Castle *(20)*, the stone at Rosemarkie Church *(3,4)*, the Boar Stone at Knocknagael (2½ miles (4km) south of Inverness) and the giant Sueno's Stone at Forres — some 20ft (7m) high, and carved all over with images from some forgotten battle.

For a while the Picts were the ascendant race in Scotland, but, although their descendants are the Scotsmen of today, their culture completely evaporated.

The name 'Scotland' is derived from the Scots — a Celtic tribe who came from Ireland about AD 500, and founded a small kingdom in Argyll, called Dalriada.

With the arrival of the Scots a pale beam of light once more illuminates Scottish history. These immigrants brought with them Gaelic, Christianity and writing, and with the last they kept the first scant records of Scottish life.

The most famous of the Scots was Columba. He was born a nobleman, but became a churchman; combining his role as a religious leader with that of a politician. In AD 565 he journeyed up the Great Glen to meet with Brude, King of the Picts, at Inverness. This trip is best remembered as the occasion of the first recorded mention of a large, unusual creature in Loch Ness, but it was successful in more ways than that. Columba had two main objectives in his embassage; firstly, to gain permission to send his acolytes throughout Pictland to establish religious foundations; and, secondly, to sue for peace for the Scots — who had been overrun by the more powerful Picts since their arrival on the west coast — to allow them to expand their territories. In the long run, the granting of the former request virtually conceded the latter. From that moment the Gaelic, Latin and Christian culture of the Scots began to replace that of the Picts. The political unification of the two nations followed in AD 843, and seems to have been a relatively bloodless business, by the extravagantly sanguine standards of the time.

The move towards unity was accelerated by the attacks of the Vikings — who had begun to trouble both nations from around AD 800 — and was sealed by a peculiarity of Pictish law: the descent of power was matrilineal. In effect, this meant that the successor to a king would not be his son, but his sister's son, or his daughter's son; thus, when the Pictish King's daughter married the Scottish King, Alpin, the resulting son, Kenneth, was heir to the crowns of both kingdoms, which he duly inherited.

The Vikings colonised the north of Scotland and the islands, but in this area they never moved south of the Black Isle in any numbers. Certainly, their paganism made little impression on the Christian Church of the area, which had flourished since the time of Columba.

The whereabouts of many of the early religious settlements are nowadays indicated by the Gaelic prefix 'kil' — 'church' — in place names. In this area, Kilmuir *(5)*, Killen and Kilcoy in the Black Isle, Kilmartin in Glen Urquhart, and others. St Moluag founded a monastic community at Rosemarkie *(3,4)*, which was later superseded by Fortrose Cathedral (completed 1485), a short distance to the west. Other religious sites in the area include the ruined Kinloss Abbey (founded 1150), the ruins of Elgin Cathedral (founded 1224), the recently rebuilt Pluscarden Abbey (founded 1230), St Benedict's Abbey and school (founded 1878), and the Victorian St Andrew's Cathedral, in Inverness (completed 1878).

By the time King Malcolm II died, in 1034, Scotland — although it lacked the islands to the north and west; still in the hands of the Norsemen — was, in extent, largely as it is today. Malcolm was a Gaelic speaking king of a Gaelic people; with the exception of the remaining Vikings and Picts in the north, a few Welsh speaking Britons in Strathclyde, and the Germanic people of Lothian. Upon his death, however, he broke with the Celtic tradition of tanistry — whereby the crown was passed between various branches of the royal family; thereby ensuring a sovereign of suitable age and ability — and gave the crown to his

daughter's son, Duncan. Not unnaturally, there was considerable displeasure among the nobles who considered themselves the rightful claimants: principally, Thorfinn the Mighty, Earl of Orkney, and MacBeth, Mormaer of Ross and Moray ('Mormaer' was an old Pictish term for a powerful regional ruler). MacBeth — who had a castle at Inverness — defeated Duncan, somewhere in Moray or the Black Isle, and killed him. He ruled Scotland (or, as the Gaelic-speakers called it, 'Alba') for seventeen years, and was generally considered a good king, before he himself was killed by Duncan's son, Malcolm Ceann Mór (*Great leader*) — a man brought up in England, who introduced many Anglo-Saxon followers, with their feudal culture and laws, in the wake of his victory.

The importance of this episode was that it marked the end of the Celtic royalty of Alba, and the start of the Anglo-Norman kingship of Scotland. The capital was moved from Dunfermline to Edinburgh — that is, from Celtic Fife to Norman Lothian. The Scottish kings now represented a minority in the kingdom, and, as a result, did not have the power to intimidate either the Celtic Highlanders, who continued to live much as they always had, or the Scottish nobles, who, by creating an alliance with anyone — French, English or Highland — could create havoc in this small, politically unbalanced country. Thus, the seeds of the problems which were to beset Scotland for the next seven centuries were set: a nobility and royalty forced into continual intrigue with foreign powers; and a people so divided by culture and language that, even in the nation's darkest moments, they could never be compelled to work together.

In the centuries following Duncan's accession the politics of the area degenerated into local power struggles. The War of Independence, which climaxed with Bruce's victory over Edward II of England at Bannockburn, in 1314, was treated by most of the Celtic families as an opportunity to gamble for gain. When Bruce began his campaign his chances of victory seemed slight, so those with the most to lose opposed him (notably, in this area, the Comyns; a family of great power, who had the added incentive that Bruce had murdered John Comyn — a rival claimant to the throne — at the start of his campaign), while those with more to gain took the gamble on Bruce, and reaped their rewards in the wake of his unexpected success. Most of the clans prominent in this area in later years came out for Bruce at Bannockburn: Fraser, Grant, Mackintosh, MacPherson and Gordon. It is worth noting that, at this time, it was still common for families to move from one side of the Highland line to the other — Fraser and Grant were both French names originally, and Gordon is a place name in the Borders; but, as time went on, the Highlands became more insular, and such movement less common.

In 1371 Bruce's line failed, and the Stewarts came to power. The early Stewarts lived in bad times, but they were not especially bad kings. They had, in varying measures, considerable wit and energy, but it was largely dissipated resolving disputes with their southern magnates. They all came to the throne young, and spent most of their reigns clearing up the mess created by a succession of regents during their minorities; before invariably dying, just as it seemed that order might be restored, and leaving the nation, once again, to the incompetent or dishonest regents. The policies which they followed in the Highlands were frequently heavy-handed, but the Stewarts had considerable Highland blood, and they seemed genuinely involved in the affairs of the north. All the Stewarts, up to Mary Queen of Scots, spoke Gaelic fluently, and remained proud of their Celtic ancestry. Their policies — generally leaving Highland affairs in the hands of one or two powerful families, who could then be played against each other to keep them from uniting against the crown — were often unpopular with their Highland subjects, but, in later years, the Highlanders remembered the

Stewarts with some affection, as the last royal house in which they could sense a measure of understanding, if not of sympathy.

It may seem strange that the Highlanders, given the purity and distinction of their culture within a strictly defined area — above the Highland Line — never formed a state of their own; particularly since there was more than enough martial power within the area to defend it against the weak Scottish crown. The nearest that the Highlanders came to such a state was under the MacDonald Lords of the Isles who, for a while, held unrestricted powers in the north and west. In 1462 a treaty was signed between John Macdonald, Lord of the Isles — styling himself as an independant ruler; the Earl of Douglas — representing the most powerful family of the southern nobility; and King Edward IV of England; agreeing to ally themselves to remove the Stewarts, and then to divide Scotland between them.

The plan was never put into operation, but the treaty was discovered, and the power of the Lordhip of the Isles waned from then on. Its court had been the centre of Gaelic culture and learning, and the only tenable power base entirely sustained from within the Highland area; so, when the Lordship of the Isles reverted to the crown in 1493 it was not simply the learning, the libraries and the records which were lost, it was also the only plausible chance of internal rule. It was never a likely occurrence in any case; the Highland society was the antithesis of the modern state: a society rooted in anarchism, not as an obscure ideal, but as a living fact. As the power of the MacDonalds grew it cast the shadow of authority over their Highland neighbours, who did not care for authority of any sort, and were among the quickest to profit when fortune turned against the MacDonalds. A great deal of idealism has been attributed to the Highlanders, but their love of personal freedom was a practical one. No clan enjoyed having powerful neighbours.

One man who wielded considerable power in this area during the early years of the Stewart dynasty was Alexander Stewart — the Wolf of Badenoch — a son of Robert II, and the king's representative in the Highlands. His main fortresses were at Lochindorb (north of Grantown-on-Spey), Ruthven (on the site of the present remains) (36) and Loch an Eilein (33). In 1390 he burnt the town and cathedral of Elgin in response to a slight from the bishop. It is worth noting that such behaviour was considered irrational and violent even at the time.

It was during this period that the clan system reached its zenith. The system was not unique to the Highlands — it was the direct descendant of the tribal divisions of the Celtic race, common, at one time, throughout central Europe — but, due to the remoteness of the Highlands, the language differences, and the lack of the will, or the strength, on the part of the Scottish monarchy, to force significant change upon the people, this archaic system lasted, in this area, into relatively modern times; the period of Empire and enlightenment.

'Clann' is the Gaelic word for 'children', but clan membership was always more flexible than that, with various families and individuals willing to give allegiance to a local chief for the safety of living within a group. The clansmen were genuinely loyal to their chiefs, but expected loyalty in return. It was not unknown for a leader to be deposed by his own people, if they felt he had proved himself unworthy.

It was a warrior society, where a chief's wealth was reckoned in men at arms; where bravery was a primary virtue, and had to be proved. In such a society life was not valued as highly as it is in our own, while honour was everything. A relatively minor insult could be the cause of a bloody and protracted feud; often lasting for generations.

This dangerous world seemed to give the people a heightened sensitivity to poetry and music, which the life of the 17th century cateran James MacPherson typifies. MacPherson was a thug — a cattle riever and

terrorist — and yet he was also a respected composer and fiddle player. Some of his compositions are still played today; including 'MacPherson's Rant' and 'MacPherson's Lament': the two pieces he played by his gallows before he was hanged (his final act was to break his fiddle across his knee; the instrument is now in the Clan MacPherson museum in Newtonmore).

A chief might reckon his wealth in men, but his finances depended on cattle. Cattle raids were a central part of Highland culture, and so were the summer and autumn cattle drives. Each year great herds of fattened beasts were driven through the hills to the lowland markets. Some of the routes in this book follow the rough tracks they used, through narrow glens and across hill passes (*12,14,32,34,35*).

The women and children of the clans lived a life of transhumance: spending their winters with the menfolk and the animals, all living together in small, dark, heather-thatched cottages in the lower glens; and, in the spring, moving with the cattle to the shielings — small huts in the high pastures. The remains of the shielings can often be seen in the higher glens. (There is a museum of Highland housing and agricultural practices in Kingussie).

In 1603, James VI became King of both Scotland and England. In the wars which coloured the reigns of the last of the Stewarts (James, Charles I, Charles II and James VI and II), the north saw much of the action. Graham of Montrose, the finest general ever to lead a Highland army, won a sequence of dazzling victories for the Catholic Charles I against the presbyterian Covenanters (including the Battle of Auldearn, near Nairn, in 1645); and Graham of Claverhouse — 'Bonnie Dundee' — was victorious for James VII at Killiecrankie. These were wars of religious ideology, but, however committed their generals were to the cause, the clans were committed only to profit and revenge. They watched to see which side their enemies joined, and joined the other.

In 1707 the Treaty of Union joined the parliaments of Scotland and England. In an independent Scotland the Highlands had been an area of considerable, ungovernable power; in the context of Great Britain it was simply a troublesome province.

By 1715 the clans were in rebellion, partly for the restoration of a Catholic, Stewart monarch (William and Mary had taken the throne of James VII in 1689) and partly in protest against the Union. The 1715 rebellion was a shambles, and, following its disintegration, General Wade was sent north from England to supervise the pacification of the Highlands. This he did, partly by raising regiments from the local population — more suited to the warfare of the terrain than were his own troops — and partly by building the first planned roads in the Highlands. These roads connected a series of forts, including Ruthven Barracks *(36)*, Fort William, Fort Augustus and Fort George, at Inverness. All of these have now disappeared with the exception of the ruins of Ruthven. Fort George was rebuilt along the coast, in 1769: it is a vast complex; still in use, but open to the public.

'General Wade's Road' is a common phrase on Highland maps: either alongside later, motor-roads, which have followed his original routes, or by the steep, hill tracks, now used only by hill walkers. The A9 follows one of his routes, as does the B862, on the south side of Loch Ness *(16)*, and the A86 from Newtonmore to Spean Bridge *(40)*. The route between Fort Augustus and Glen Moriston *(14)* follows a later military road.

The Highlanders were not at all happy to have their glens made more accessible — their strongest defence had always been inaccessibility — but the roads proved a great boon to later travellers. In the words of the famous couplet: '*Had you seen these roads before they were made, / You would lift up your hands and bless General Wade!*'

There was a second Jacobite rising in 1745. The Stewart cause depended on the support of

the Catholic clans, and of those others who wished to strike at the hand of Hanoverian authority. The most powerful clans of the time, in this area, were the MacPhersons, in upper Strathspey; the Grants, in lower Strathspey; the Mackintoshes of Strath Dearn and Strath Nairn; the Frasers of Loch Ness and the Aird; the Chisholms of Glen Affric; and the Mackenzies, who held land in the Black Isle. (Minor families included the Shaws, McBains, MacGillivrays of Strath Nairn *(18)* and MacQueens of Strath Dearn *(19)* — all part of the loosely related Clan Chattan Confederacy, under the leadership of the Makintoshes.) The farmland of Nairn and Moray was owned by a number of smaller estates. It is difficult to make snap statements about who supported the Jacobite cause and who did not — many of the clans were divided — however, the Grants were broadly Hanoverian, and the balance broadly Jacobite. The Mackintoshes serve as an example of the divisions. The clan chief held a commission in the Black Watch — one of the government's Highland regiments — and remained Hanoverian throughout. His wife, on the other hand — 'Colonel Anne' — was a Jacobite, and raised a force from the clan for the Stewarts.

In all, only 6000 Highlanders joined the Stewart cause — evidence of a general scepticism — but all the clans, Jacobite and Hanoverian alike, were punished in the aftermath of a battle which ended not only the rebellion, but also the power of the clans — Culloden. The battle site is a few miles to the east of Inverness, and is maintained by the National Trust for Scotland. It is a forlorn spot; a monument to a battle where nothing was won, and a whole way of life was lost.

Prince Charles Edward Stewart fled the battlefield and, after many adventures, the country. The selfless courage shown by many Highlanders, both supporters and opponents, in effecting his escape was quite remarkable. Similarly touching is the loyalty shown by the people of the clan MacPherson. Their chief, a

leading Jacobite, was hunted by the government troops. He hid for nine years in a cave (on Creag Dubh, near Newtonmore) without being given away, despite the offer of a vast reward for his capture.

The hardships endured by the Highlanders at the hands of the victorious Hanoverian army, led by the Duke of Cumberland, were compounded by the insults of the ensuing legislation. Not only was the Disarming Act — first introduced after the '15 — reinforced, but the people were banned from wearing the Highland tartans, under the threat of deportation. In addition, no effort was spared to impress upon the people the inferiority of their language and lifestyle.

There is very little in this area to add substance to the history of the Highlanders. A few of the larger castles remain — the ruins of Urquhart Castle, by the side of Loch Ness; Cawdor and Brodie *(20)* on the farmland east of Inverness; Castle Grant, in Grantown-on-Spey — but little was built to last in a land where destruction was a way of life.

Following Culloden, many of the clan chiefs, needing to establish themselves under the new regime, raised regiments from their clansmen, to fight for the Hanoverians. These regiments acquitted themselves with great bravery, and disproportionate loss, in Europe and America, for a country which was only too glad to see the back of them.

This was also the sentiment of an increasing number of clan chiefs, who were now — deprived of their ancient powers and responsi- bilities — little more than landlords of vast, unprofitable estates. Their need was more for money than for men.

All the Highland towns are products of this period: clearance towns, built to take the overspill when the glens were cleared of men and cattle to make way for sheep — more profitable tenants of the land.

Many Highlanders, unwilling to accept the new conditions, and often financially encouraged by their chiefs, emigrated; usually to a better

life. Others, not wishing to leave the country, moved to the new harbours along the coast (in this area: Lossiemouth, Hopeman and Burghead), and took to the herring fishery; a hard and dangerous life, chasing the 'silver darlings' in an open boat. Others took jobs building the roads and railways or — at the start of the 19th century — Telford's Caledonian Canal (7).

The suppression of the spirit of the remaining Highlanders was so swift and successful that, within a hundred years of Culloden, the Highlands were safe enough to have become fashionable.

The transformation was largely triggered by a gradual appreciation of the bravery and effectiveness of the Highland regiments, and also by the work of James 'Ossian' MacPherson — the successful perpetrator of one of the finest literary frauds of all time. MacPherson was born at Ruthven (36) in 1736, and worked, for a while, as a tutor. In 1760 he published his first 'translations' of ancient Gaelic epics, originally written by the 3rd century bard, Ossian. Folk tales of Ossian and the Fingalian warriors were common enough in Scotland and Ireland, but MacPherson's epics, in their turgid, hollow English, were all his own work. His tales of misty heroism were extraordinarily popular. His work was compared to Homer's; it swept across Europe, influencing Goethe, inspiring Napoleon, and signalling the start of the Romantic movement. In addition, it

brought its author a seat in parliament, a large estate on Speyside and a burial in Westminster Abbey. There is a monument to this most successful and least read of Scottish authors at Balavil, near Kingussie.

The romanticising of the Highlands was completed by Queen Victoria and Prince Albert, who purchased Balmoral Castle, in Deeside, in 1852. They made tartan and pipe-bands fashionable, and started a vogue for Highland holidays which led directly to the development of the north-south rail links and the growth of the towns along the lines. At the same time the estates, which were now owned by men who made their fortunes outside the Highlands, and who could afford to maintain the lands for leisure, were turned into sporting estates, with deer stalking, grouse shooting and salmon fishing.

These estates are still in operation today, as are the fishing ports and the sheep farms. More recently developed forms of employment include commercial forestry — which is rife throughout the area — hydro-electric power and the expansion of the tourist industry — including the development of the winter sports facilities in the Cairngorms.

One other old industry has lasted the years. The place names of lower Speyside should be music to the ear of any whisky drinker, for this area has the greatest concentration of malt distilleries in the country.

C Place Names

The original meanings of place names are often obscured by time and language. This problem is particularly acute in the north where place names are derived from at least five separate cultures: pre-Celtic, Pictish, Scandinavian, Gaelic and English. The names of the larger rivers — Spey, Findhorn, Ness etc — would seem to be the most antiquated, being derived from roots common throughout Europe, and predating the Celtic peoples. They are totally obscure.

Surviving Pictish names are rare, but the geographical range of this people throughout Scotland, when they existed as a separate race, can be accurately traced by one particular prefix — 'pit' — which is a Pictish word signifying a piece of land and seems to have been adopted by the later Gaelic people to distinguish originally Pictish settlements — eg, 'Pitmain' (near Kingussie), 'Pittendreich' (near Elgin) and others.

Scandinavian place names, brought by the Vikings, are rare in this area, but there are some, generally distorted or blended with Gaelic elements, in the Black Isle — eg, 'Udale' and 'Culbo'.

The Scots names (ie, of the Scots or 'Lallans' dialect of English) are commonest on the coastal plain of Moray, and the further east one looks the commoner they become. This is because the people of the eastern areas changed from speaking Gaelic to speaking Scots at an earlier period than did those of the western areas. Later still, English speaking landowners began providing names. Moray contains the full range — eg, 'Carn na Cailliche' (Gaelic), 'Hempriggs' and 'Paddockhaugh' (Scots) and 'Newton' and 'Charlestown' (English).

By far the greatest number of names in this area are of Gaelic origin. A list of the commonest elements in Gaelic place names is given below, but don't be surprised if the map spelling differs from that shown below: this is due partly to the anglicisation of the words and partly to Gaelic grammar, which causes nouns and adjectives to alter, depending on their use in the sentence. One final tip. In Gaelic the adjective generally follows the noun: eg, 'Cairngorm' — Blue Hill, 'Monadhliath' — Grey Moor.

Translations are given of place names in the text, where they are of particular interest.

Common Gaelic Elements in Place Names

Aber — *Confluence*
Abhainn — *River*
Achadh, Ach, Auch — *Field*
Allt — *Stream*
Ard — *High*
Bal, Ball — *Town, settlement*
Ban — *White, Pale*
Beag, Beg — *Small*
Beinn, Ben — *Mountain*
Beith — *Birch*
Blair — *Level field*
Breac — *Speckled*
Buidhe — *Yellow*
Cam — *Bent*
Caoruinn — *Rowan*
Carn, Cairn — *Hill, heap of stones*
Ceann, Kin — *Head*
Clach — *Stone*
Cladh — *Burial place*
Cnoc — *Hillock*
Coille — *Wood*
Coire, Corrie — *Kettle, hollow*
Craggan — *Rocky hillock*
Creag, Craig — *Rock, cliff*
Croit, Croft — *Highland smallholding*

Cruaidh, Croy — *Hard*
Dal, Dail — *Meadow*
Darach — *Oak*
Dearg — *Red*
Donn — *Brown*
Doire — *Grove*
Druim, Drum — *Ridge*
Dubh — *Black*
Dun — *Steep hill*
Eas, Ess — *Waterfall*
Eilean — *Island*
Elrig — *Deer Trap*
Fearn — *Alder*
Feith — *Bog*
Fionn — *White, fair*
Garbh — *Rough*
Garadh — *Enclosure*
Geal — *White, bright*
Glas — *Grey/green*
Gleann, Glen — *Valley*
Gobhar, Gower — *Goat*
Gorm — *Blue*
Innis, Inch — *Island*
Inver — *River mouth*
Kil — *Church*
Lagan, Laggan — *Hollow*
Lairig — *Hill pass*

Leacann, Lechkin — *Slope*
Leitir, Letter — *Extensive slope*
Liath — *Grey*
Lochan — *Small loch*
Mam — *Large round hill*
Meadhonach — *Middle*
Meall — *Lump, shapeless hill*
Moine — *Moss, peat*
Monadh — *Extensive hill, moorland*
Mor — *Large*
Ros — *Promontory*
Ruadh — *Red*
Sgeir — *Skerry*
Sgurr — *Peak, sharp top*
Sneachd — *Snow*
Strath — *Wide valley*
Sron, Strone — *Nose, point*
Stac — *Rocky column, cliff*
Stob — *Point, peak*
Stuc — *Pinnacle*
Tigh — *House*
Tir — *Land*
Tomb, Tom — *Hillock*
Tulach, Tullich — *Knoll*
Uaine — *Green*
Uamh — *Cave*
Uisge — *Water*

D Natural History

Some of the more exotic animals which once roamed the area have now gone, and all of the more dangerous ones: the **lynx** at the dawn of man's habitation; the **auroch** (a wild ox), **brown bear** and **reindeer** (now reintroduced) in his early history; the **great elk** in the 14th century; **beaver** and **wild boar** in the 16th century; and the last **wolf** in the mid 18th century. In addition, a number of the larger birds have gone — the **capercaillie** and **osprey** (both now reintroduced) and **red kite**. A formidable list still remains, however, and a number of species of birds and animals exist in the north of Scotland which cannot be found elsewhere in Britain.

The plant life is also unique in some aspects, due to the peculiar conditions of the high mountain plateaux, extensive moorland and pine forests.

The area can usefully be divided into a number of distinct environments, which recur along the various routes in this book — **Caledonian Pine Forest, Commercial Forestry, Broad-leaved Woodland, Mountain and Moorland, Farmland, Freshwater, Seashore** — and the bird, animal and plant species typical of each environment can then be listed. This has been done below. Routes which particularly feature each environment are listed beside the headings, while those which are most likely to provide a view of a particular species (if the species is rare enough to require such distinction) are listed beside the species name. Naturally, it is impossible to be entirely accurate with such a brief study, and great good fortune is required to see some of the rarer and shyer species, but this should give a rough indication of what may be seen along the way.

Caledonian Pine Forest *(11,12,25,30,32,33)*

The **Scots pine** is the only conifer indigenous to the British Isles, and forests containing little else once covered much of the Scottish Highlands — at one time up to a height of 3000ft (900m) above sea level. Nowadays the natural forest exists only in a few small, protected pockets between 700 and 1500ft (200-750m). In this area the main forests are around the Cairngorms in the south, and in Glen Affric in the west.

The disappearance of the original forests was due partly to clearance for timber and farmland and partly to climatic changes, which seem to have reduced the pine's ability to regenerate — it is not uncommon to see stands of old trees with no younger trees coming through beneath them. In these remaining, protected areas of Caledonian forest, regeneration is being encouraged, and, where it is proving slow, random planting is being undertaken to maintain the tree cover.

The **Scots pine** is distinguished by its pale pink/brown bark, and by the dark, bottle green of its needles. In its early years it grows straight and conical, like a spruce, but later, given the space to spread out, it can develop into a number of shapes — sometimes spreading from the top of a long, straight trunk; sometimes sprouting from low on the bole. The tree often develops into dramatic and contorted forms, particularly when exposed to the wind. In areas of shallow soil, with a shortage of nutrients, or near or above the tree line, where the temperature is rarely high enough to allow growth, the tree, though often quite old, remains stunted.

A typical Caledonian pine forest consists almost entirely of the one species of tree, interspersed with **birch, rowan** and **alder. Birch** is particularly common in the damp conditions of Glen Affric.

Beneath the trees is a thick mat of **bell** and **ling heather, blaeberry, cowberry** and various mosses. In the Speyside forests there is also considerable **juniper** — a dark springy shrub which can grow in low thickets, or as a single plant, up to 25ft (7.5m) in height.

The forest contains a wide array of the smaller birds: **blue, great** and **coal tits, treecreeper, bullfinch, chaffinch** and **wren,** as well as the more particular **goldcrest** and **siskin,**

and the localised conifer specialists: **crested tit** and **Scottish crossbill** *(25,30,32,33)*.

Of the larger birds, the most spectacular is the **capercaillie** — the largest of the native grouse — which had died out in the Highlands but was reintroduced in the early 20th century. It is now quite common in the pine forests. The cock is large, black and not unlike a turkey; but it is more likely to be heard, crashing through the branches of trees, than seen.

There is not a great deal of animal life peculiar to the forest, but **roe** and **red deer** are likely to be seen — the latter only during the colder months, when they come down from the hills in search of grazing. **Red squirrels** are common in this area. Of the carnivores, **fox, badger, stoat, wildcat** and **weasel** all inhabit the forest, but only the last two are likely to be seen. The **pine marten,** once nearly extinct and still rare, lives in the forests of Glen Affric *(11,12).*

Commercial Forestry *(8,9,13,14,15,17,18,20, 21,24,27,29,30,32,34,35,39,40)*

Compared with the Caledonian forest, the more extensive commercial plantations are comparatively uninteresting for naturalists. There is very little undergrowth, due to the lack of light reaching the forest floor, and the animal life is similarly scarce — although **roe** and **red deer** are both seen along the forest tracks. The bird life is largely that of the Caledonian forest, but the birds are harder to see in the dense woodland.

The major interest is in the variety of conifer types which are now planted. The list includes **Scots pine; Sitka** and **Norway spruce; Japanese, European** and **hybrid larch; Douglas fir; western red hemlock** and a great many others. Most of the routes listed above pass through entirely commercial plantations, but in some the conifers are older, and widely spaced. These are maintained as beauty spots *(9,13,17,24).*

Broad-leaved Woodland *(4,28)*

Although only two of the routes are listed as passing through predominantly broad-leaved woodland, most of them pass through some. The commonest species of broad-leaved trees in this area are **birch, rowan, alder** and **oak,** although **beech, ash, hawthorn, holly** and others also appear. The greatest variety of trees is on the warmer, coastal belt by the Moray Firth. In the highlands **birch,** which grows up to 2000ft (600m), is by far the commonest broad-leaved tree. Craigellachie Wood *(28)* is entirely of **birch,** and is maintained as a nature reserve.

A great variety of grasses, flowers, mosses, and lichens grow in these woods, while large areas — particularly in the birch woods — are covered by **bracken.**

Most of the larger mammals exist in woodland throughout the area, the **rabbit, fox, badger, hedgehog, weasel, stoat** and **roe deer** of the lower woods being supplemented by the **wildcat** and **red deer** (in the colder months) in the higher wooded glens.

A wide variety of tits, warblers, pipits and finches inhabit the woods; the **long-tailed tit** being particularly drawn to the **birch** woods. In addition, **woodcock, mistle** and **song thrush, blackbird** and **wren** are likely to be seen. **Buzzard** and **Kestrel** also nest in these woods.

Mountains and Moorland *(12,14,18,30,31,35,36,37,38)*

The Highlands are famous for their moors: vast areas of heather which give a purple shade to the hillsides from July to September. They seem empty, yet these moors are of considerable interest to naturalists, and are a central part of the local economy — as sheep runs, grouse moors and deer forests — so be careful not to disturb the wildlife, and always check with estates, tourist information centres and local people before walking on the moors from August onwards, when grouse shooting and deer stalking are in progress.

The plant life which constitutes the moors varies greatly, depending on which direction the moor slopes, its height above sea level, and the underlying rock or soil. Flat areas of moorland are often 'floating' on a considerable depth of peat: a mass of black, sodden, half rotted vegetation, which provides effective fuel when dried. These peat moors tend to be very wet (16,38), and pools and bogs of dark water often develop. These encourage plants such as **bog cotton, bog asphodel** and the pungent **bog myrtle.** For the most part, however, the moors are predominantly of **ling heather,** with **bell heather, blaeberry** and other shrubs intermixed. On the mountain slopes the **ling** gives way to a covering of **blaeberry, crowberry, dwarf juniper** and others.

Parts of the moor are burnt in the spring, to encourage new growth in the heather to feed the **red grouse. Grouse** are common up to 3000ft (900m), and are frequently seen springing up from the heather and flying off swiftly, giving a strange, nasal call, generally transcribed as *'go back, go back, go back'.* Other birds to be seen on the lower moors include the **skylark, stonechat, wheatear** and **curlew.** Crows are present here, as everywhere: both the **carrion** and the grey cowled **hooded crow.**

The red deer are high in the hills during the summer — partly to escape the fierce insect life of the summer moors — but return to the lower moors in the autumn, and can often be seen from the main roads during the winter. **Wildcat, fox** and **stoat** are present, although generally unseen, along with the **blue hare** — slightly smaller than the common variety — which, like the stoat, turns white during the winter months.

Another creature which camouflages itself against the winter snow fields by turning white is the **ptarmigan** (31), This bird — the hardiest of the grouse family — will only venture below 2500ft (750m) in the severest winter weather, otherwise remaining on the sub-arctic hilltops. These hilltops — particularly in the Cairngorms — are an example of how much of Scotland must have looked some 10,000 years ago, just after the last ice age. No plant can grow to any size, because of the extremely short growing season and the high winds, so the cover is of dwarf shrubs, sheltering between the broken rocks of the summits. Apart from the **ptarmigan,** few birds exist at this height, but the Cairngorms (31) have a few **dotterel** and **snow bunting** near the peaks.

One creature which existed in Scotland until the 9th century — the **reindeer** — has been reintroduced, and grazes on the lichens in the Cairngorms. These are quite tame and harmless.

The commonest of the birds of prey throughout the area is the **buzzard,** but there is always a chance of seeing a **kestrel, peregrine** or **merlin** on the moors; or even, in the more remote glens, a **golden eagle.**

Farmland (1,2,10,19)

The farmland around the Moray Firth is varied — livestock and crops — and well interspersed with natural woodland, windbreaks and conifer plantations. The wildlife tends to consist of overspills from such woodland reservoirs. Most of the woodland birds, previously mentioned, are present, along with the **robin, yellowhammer** and **greenfinch.** In addition there are **curlew** and **lapwing** on the rougher pasture, and large flocks of **redwing** and **fieldfare** during the autumn and winter.

Farm animals apart, the mammals tend to be small: **voles, bats, mice** and **shrews, stoat** and **weasel.**

Flowers in the ditches, hedgerow, pasture land and woodland are abundant and varied.

Freshwater (4,6,7,9,15,20,24,25,26,29,33,34,35,37)

This is rather a broad grouping, incorporating low level lochs, hill burns and moorland peat bogs. A great deal of water falls on the Highlands, eventually reaching the sea via a teeming network of bogs, burns, ponds, falls, lochans, lochs and rivers, so most of the routes in this book pass likely habitats along the way

— only those routes where the water is a central feature are listed above.

The **bog cotton, asphodel** and **myrtle** and various mosses of the peat bogs give way to largely woodland plants as the small burns pass through their high-sided, narrow glens *(4,9,13)*. Various pondweeds, reeds, sedges and grasses are common by the lochs and lochans, along with **water lily, water lobelia** and others.

The most famous of Scottish water birds — the **osprey** — nests in this area. This splendid bird is no longer as rare as it once was, and can be seen fishing at many of the lochs throughout the area. There is a hide at the nesting site on Loch Garten *(25)*.

Duck are very common at all stages of the rivers' development, with **mallard** and **teal** as high as the moor's edge, and **wigeon, pochard, goldeneye, red-breasted merganser, tufted duck** and **goosander** in the lower waters.

Also by the upper waters are **redshank, curlew** and **lapwing**; while **dippers** and **grey** and **pied wagtails** are common in the shaded dens *(4,9,13)*.

None of the routes in this book passes close to the nesting areas of the **red-throated** or **black-throated diver** — the high lochans, specifically chosen for their isolation — but both species nest within this area, and may be seen flying overhead.

The variety of freshwater fish in the area is not great, but those species which do exist do so in great numbers. The most common of all is the **brown trout** — resident in most bodies of water — and the most important is the **Atlantic salmon,** which ascends the rivers during the summer, to spawn in the headwaters at the end of the year. These fish can be seen jumping in rivers throughout the area, the Spey being a particularly noted salmon river. In the lochs there are **pike** and **perch** in great numbers, **eels** and, in the deeper lochs, **char** — a distant cousin of the **salmon.**

There are few mammals which specifically live by the water, but one — the **otter** — is not uncommon throughout the area, although it is quite rare to see one. Other swimmers include **water vole** and **mink.** Also, since the 6th century, there have been reports of something a little larger living in Loch Ness. Such reports are unsubstantiated, if intriguing, and the debate about the 'Loch Ness Monster' has yet to be concluded.

Seashore *(1,2,3,5,22)*

The seashore in this area is composed of the cliffs *(1,3,5)* and mud flats *(2,5)* of the Black Isle, and the cliffs and long sand beaches of the Moray coast *(22)*.

The plant life of the shore includes lichens and seaweeds, and a variety of small plants inured to the salty conditions, such as **sea pink, sea milkwort, scurvy grass, red fescue** and **marram.** The **marram** is particularly important along the Moray coasts, where it binds the sand dunes and stops them from creeping inland.

There are very few mammals along the shore, but a great many crustaceans: **limpets, whelks, barnacles** and others.

The great glory of the Moray Firth, however, is the birdlife. In winter, particularly, there are tremendous numbers of waders and ducks on the mud flats of the Black Isle *(2,5)*, including **oystercatcher, curlew, dunlin, knot, bar-tailed godwit, ringed plover** and **redshank; shelduck, eider, wigeon, pochard, tufted duck, scaup, goldeneye, long-tailed duck, red-breasted merganser, goosander, common scoter, teal** and **mallard.** In addition there are **grey lag** and **pink footed geese** and **mute** and **whooper swans.** Other residents of the foreshore include **gulls, terns, cormorant** and **heron.** A tremendous collection.

General

Many of these species are shy and sensitive to intrusion, so it is important to disturb them as little as possible. The walker is in no danger from the wildlife of the area, although, as a general rule, it is wise to stay clear of any creature with young.

Of the domestic animals, **sheep-dogs** can be a nuisance, but are generally bluffing; **bulls**, on the other hand, should never be approached, however lethargic they may appear.

There is one poisonous snake in the area — the **adder**. It is rare to see one — usually coiled in a patch of sunlight, somewhere quiet — and even rarer to be bitten. **Adders** are extremely shy and will always move if they sense anyone approaching. Anyone who is bitten should consult a doctor. Bites are not lethal, but they give rise to an unpleasant, temporary illness.

Two insects are deserving of note. The **cleg,** or horse fly, is very common, particularly in moorland areas, and delivers an irritating bite. Even more numerous, and the bane of the outdoor enthusiast's life, is the **midge.** These diminutive insects tend to congregate around water, but, since water is virtually omnipresent in this area, they are rather difficult to avoid. There are a number of creams and sprays to deter them, but they generally find a way through the best prepared defences. Midges are particularly active around sunset.

E Advice to Walkers

Always check the weather forecast before setting off on the longer walks and prepare yourself for the walk accordingly. Remember that an excess of sunshine — causing sunburn or dehydration — can be just as debilitating as snow or rain, and carry adequate cover for your body in all conditions when on the hills.

Snow cover on the higher slopes often remains well into the summer and should be avoided by inexperienced walkers as it often covers hidden watercourses and other pitfalls which are likely to cause injury. Also, when soft, snow is extremely gruelling to cross and can sap the energy very quickly. Walking on snow-covered hills should not be attempted without an ice-axe and crampons.

The other weather-associated danger on the hills is the mist, which can appear very swiftly and cut visibility to a few yards. Such conditions should be anticipated, and a map and compass carried while on the higher hills.

Obviously these problems are unlikely to arise on the shorter, simpler routes, but it is always wise when out walking to anticipate the worst and to be ready for it. The extra equipment may never be needed, but it is worth taking anyway, just in case. Spare food, a first-aid kit, a whistle and a torch with a spare battery should be carried on all hill walks. In addition, details of your route and expected time of return should be left with

someone, whom you should advise on your safe return.

There is one final danger for hill walkers which is entirely predictable. From August onwards there is grouse shooting and deer stalking on the moors. If you are undertaking one of the hill routes then check with the local estate or tourist officer before doing so, thereby avoiding a nuisance for the sportsmen and possible danger to yourself.

Country Code

All walkers, when leaving public roads to pass through farmland, forestry or moorland, should respect the interests of those whose livelihood depends on the land. Carelessness can easily cause damage. You are therefore urged to follow the Country Code:

Guard against all risk of fire
Keep all dogs under proper control
   (especially during the lambing season —
   April/May)
Fasten all gates
Keep to the paths across farmland
Avoid damaging fences, hedges and walls
Leave no litter
Safeguard water supplies
Protect wildlife, wild plants and trees
Go carefully on country roads
Respect the life of the countryside

1 Cromarty

Length: 3½ miles (5.5km) there and back
Height climbed: 400ft (110m)
Grade: C
Public conveniences: Cromarty
Public transport: Bus service from Inverness

Leisurely walk on metalled roads, leading to a splendid view of the Cromarty Firth and the North Sea.

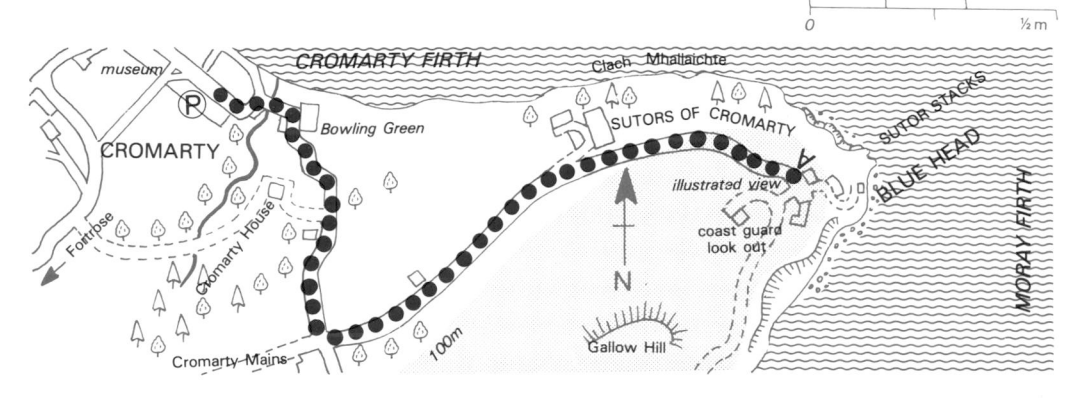

The north of Scotland is not noted for the charm of its towns, so Cromarty, on the tip of the Black Isle, comes as a pleasant surprise. To reach the town, from Inverness, cross the Kessock Bridge and then turn right onto the Munlochy road, and then right again, onto the A832. Cromarty was once a port of some importance, but now the quiet, narrow streets are in considerable contrast to the industrial activity at Nigg Bay, one mile away, across the Cromarty Firth.

This route starts from the eastern end of the town, following a narrow metalled road, past the bowling club and up a shallow hill. Hidden in the woods to the right of this road is the 18th century Cromarty House. An odd feature of this building is a tunnel, leading from the gate to the building.

Beyond the house the road continues to Cromarty Mains Farm. Turn left here, and continue climbing, up to the cliff-top gun emplacements overlooking the mouth of the firth — relics of the last world war. The view from here is superb (see below).

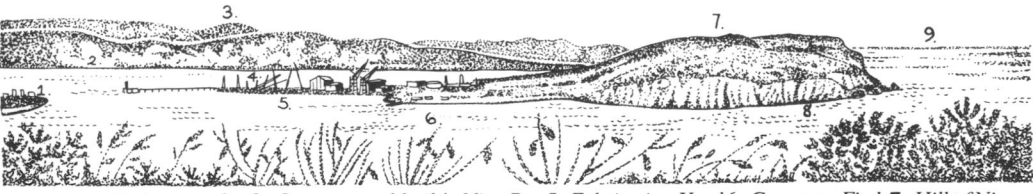

1. *Cromarty* 2. *Invergordon* 3. *Cnoc an t-sabhail* 4. *Nigg Bay* 5. *Fabrication Yard* 6. *Cromarty Firth* 7. *Hill of Nigg* 8. *North Sutor* 9. *Moray Firth*

2 Udale Bay

Length: 2 miles (3km)
Height climbed: 110ft (35m)
Grade: C
Public conveniences: None
Public transport: Bus service between Inverness and Cromarty; runs through Jemimaville

Mud flats may not be everyone's idea of the perfect view, but the shallows of Udale Bay are of great interest to bird watchers. A great many waders and ducks choose to winter here.

To reach the walk from Inverness cross the Kessock Bridge and turn right, on to the road to Fortrose, then turn left on to the B9610 at the top of the glen behind Rosemarkie. Park opposite the ruined St Michael's chapel.

Start the walk along the side of Udale Bay. It is unwise to venture on to the mud, which is very soft.

From Newhallpoint there is a particularly fine view (see below) across the Cromarty Firth. To the north-west are Ben Wyvis and the surrounding hills; to the east is the mouth of the firth, between Nigg and Cromarty. The area is of great importance to the oil industry — there is a platform construction yard at Nigg Bay — and there is usually a platform or two anchored in the firth.

Turn left up to Balblair and then left again, along the B9163, to return to the chapel.

A short walk on quiet public roads, with views across the mud flats of Udale Bay — rich in bird life — and across the Cromarty Firth.

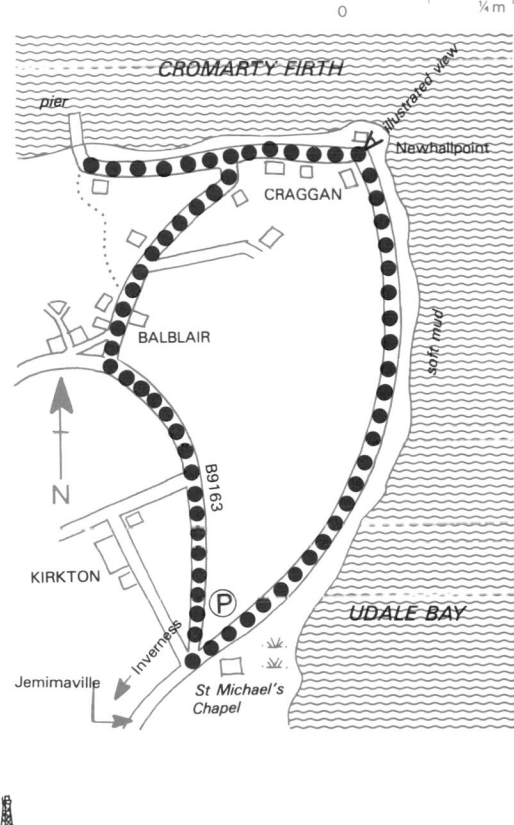

1. *Invergordon* 2. *Cromarty Firth* 3. *Nigg Bay* 4. *Hill of Nigg* 5. *Udale Bay* 6. *Moray Firth* 7. *Cromarty* 8. *The Black Isle*

3 Rosemarkie Cliffs

Length: 3 miles (5km) there and back
Height climbed: None
Grade: B
Public conveniences: Rosemarkie
Public transport: Bus service between Inverness and Cromarty

A coastal walk on sand and rocks, with cliffs, caves, seabirds and fine views across the Moray Firth.

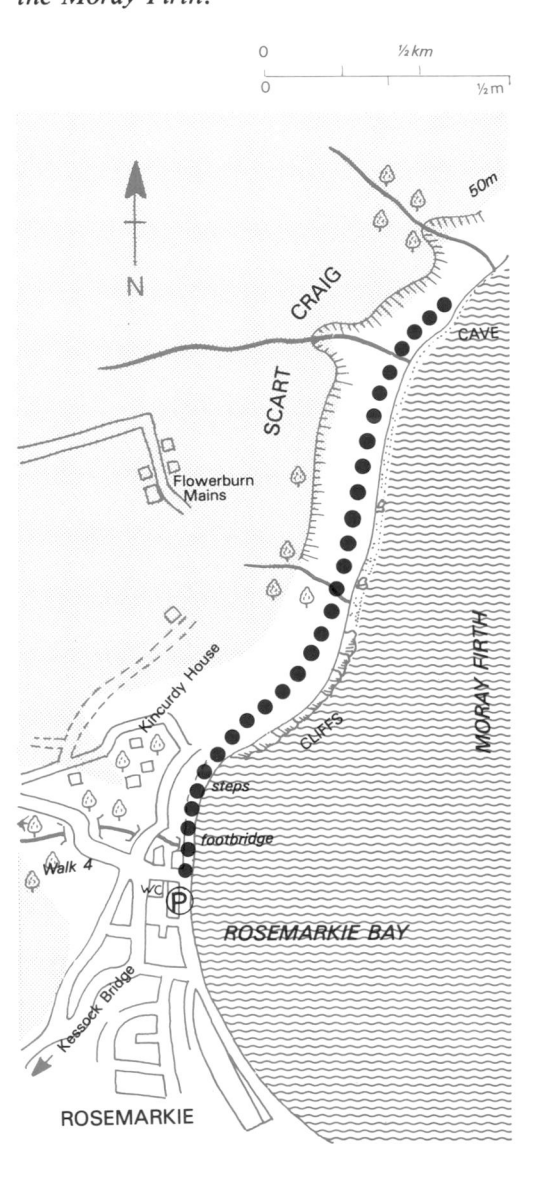

To reach Rosemarkie from Inverness, cross the Kessock Bridge, turn right, and then follow the signs: first for Munlochy and then for Rosemarkie. There is space for parking on the promenade.

The first part of the walk is on a clear path: across a footbridge over a small burn, up some steps, and along a wooded path above the beach. The path then gradually descends to the foreshore, notable for its pink sand and cliffs.

Along this stretch of coast there are fine views of the Moray Firth. To the right (west) is Chanonry Point with its lighthouse, jutting out beyond Rosemarkie. Almost meeting it, from the opposite side of the firth, is the cape of Fort George. Originally, this imposing 18th century barrack — designed by Robert Adam and covering 12 acres — was intended to help quell the rebellious clans in the north. Nowadays it is still garrisoned by the Highland regiments.

To the left (east) of the fort is Whiteness Head, with its oil platform construction yard.

At the end of the beach are the cliffs of Scart Craig and a very fine cave. The shore curves round to the mud flats of Munlochy Bay beyond the point, but be careful not to be cut off beyond the point by the rising tide.

4 The Fairy Glen

Length: 2 miles (3km) there and back
Height climbed: 150ft (40m)
Grade: C
Public conveniences: Rosemarkie
Public transport: Bus service between Inverness and Cromarty

A short walk up a wooded glen, with views of small waterfalls. Path good until the first fall and then tricky.

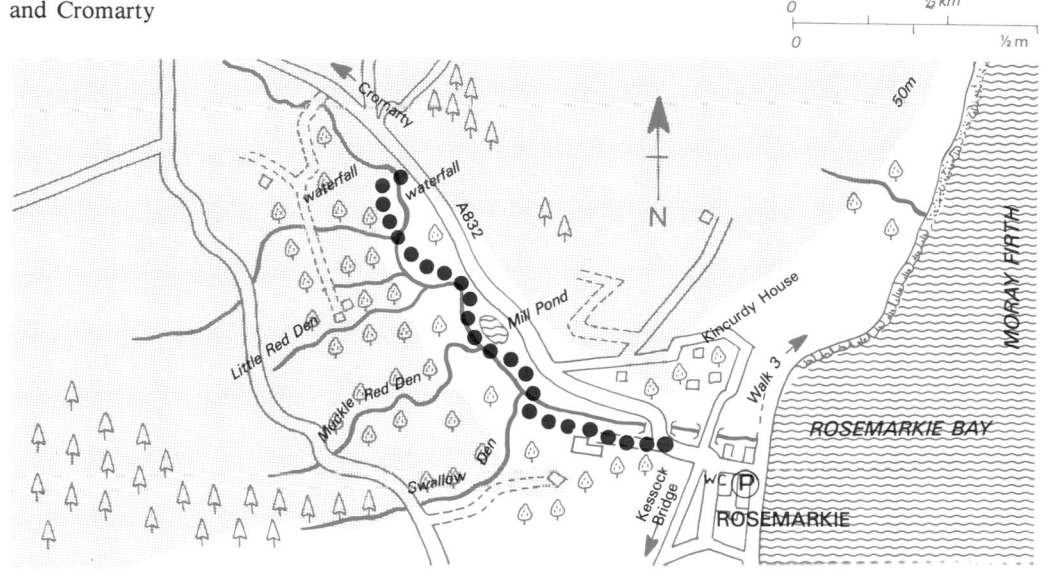

This walk follows a very pleasant den — a narrow, wooded glen   to two sets of waterfalls near its head.

To reach Rosemarkie from Inverness, cross the Kessock Bridge, turn right on the road to Munlochy, and then right again, on the A832. There is a car park at the foot of the glen, just beyond the sharp bend at the Plough Inn.

Follow the public road a short distance, to the bridge over the burn, and turn left, before the bridge, on to a footpath. The way is quite clear from now on.

The glen — free of grazing animals — is full of broad-leaved woodland, and the air is very

cool beneath the high canopy of leaves. Note how thin the tree trunks are — the trees need to grow very tall very quickly in order to make the most of the limited sunlight.

After the first fall the path becomes less flat — clambering over rocks, often made slippery by the spray of the burn. It is worth the effort, however. The top fall drops into a very pleasant wide, shallow, shady basin, overhung by trees.

Return by the same route or climb the bank and cut right, on to the A832, and return to Rosemarkie by that route.

5 Kilmuir

Length: 3 miles (5km) there and back
Height climbed: None
Grade: B
Public conveniences: None
Public transport: None

A quiet coastal walk, along faint tracks and the rocky foreshore. Caves, cliffs and all the associated wildlife.

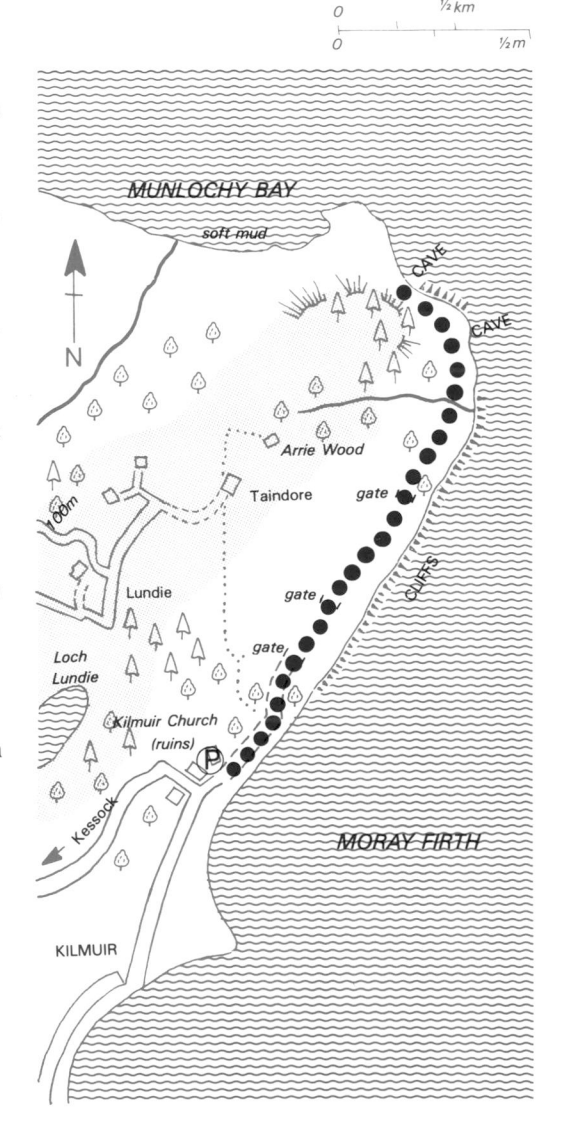

Kilmuir is a pleasant little hamlet near the southern tip of the Black Isle. To reach it from Inverness take the A9 north, over the Kessock Bridge, and then take the first turning to the right. The second right, right at the T-junction and first left. The walk starts a little before the road reaches the village. At a hairpin bend there are some empty farm buildings — park here. Just next door are the ruins of Kilmuir Church, probably dating from the 15th century.

The path continues past the church and through some sparse woodland towards the shore. There are fine views all along this walk: across the Moray Firth to the low coastline east of Inverness, and east to the point of Fort George, jutting in to the firth, with Chanonry Ness opposite it on the Black Isle side.

The walk continues across farmland with grazing animals, on a low, broad step, between a steep escarpment to the left and a sharp drop to the sea on the right. Go through another gate. The path now becomes a little unclear, as it pushes through dense undergrowth, before reaching the shore.

There is a great deal of bird life along the shoreline. Watch particularly for cormorants on this stretch. Oystercatchers, curlews and herons are also common.

The hill to the left becomes steeper as the path rounds the point of Craigiehowe. Set into the cliff is a large cave.

A little further around the point there is a view into Munlochy Bay. The extensive mud flats here are a great attraction for waterfowl and waders.

Return by the same route.

6 Inverness Islands

Length: 2 miles (3km)
Height climbed: None
Grade: C
Public conveniences: Inverness
Public transport: Regular bus and train services
to Inverness from every direction

*A short walk along the banks of the River
Ness, in Inverness, including a path across
a small group of wooded islands.*

For some time Inverness has prospered as the
administrative centre for the remote country of
the north and west. It was the area's Pictish
capital when St Columba visited King Brude
here in AD 565. However, the site was
inhabited long before that and has remained
so, with increasing importance, ever since.
Inverness is now the home of the administrative
offices of the largest of Britain's regions —
Highland. The headquarters of the Highlands
and Islands Development Board are also here.

The centrepiece of the town is the winding,
grass-banked River Ness, with its pedestrian
suspension bridges and wooded islands — this
is much the prettiest part of the town. Start
walking at the junction of Bridge Street and
Castle Road. Along this first stretch Inverness
Castle sits on the hill to the left of the path.
This neat but rather uninspiring building —
the most recent of many on the site — was
completed in 1846 to replace the castle
destroyed by the Jacobites in 1746. It houses
administration offices.

The way continues along Ness Bank and
Lady's Walk to the first of the islands. There
are two large islands, with a number of smaller
ones scattered around them. They are quiet,
pleasant parks, with a wide variety of tree
types, and are connected to each other, and to
the banks of the river, by a series of
footbridges.

Walk down the west bank, along Ness Walk,
past the modern Eden Court Theatre, and St
Mary's Episcopal Cathedral (1878). The latter
was the masterpiece of the local architect
Alexander Ross.

Continue down Ness Walk and turn right
across the bridge, to return to the starting
point.

7 Caledonian Canal

Length: Up to 10 miles (16km)
Height climbed: None
Grade: A/B/C
Public conveniences: Inverness
Public transport: Bus and train services to Inverness from every direction

A long flat walk by the side of the canal, through woodland, farmland and residential areas along the banks.

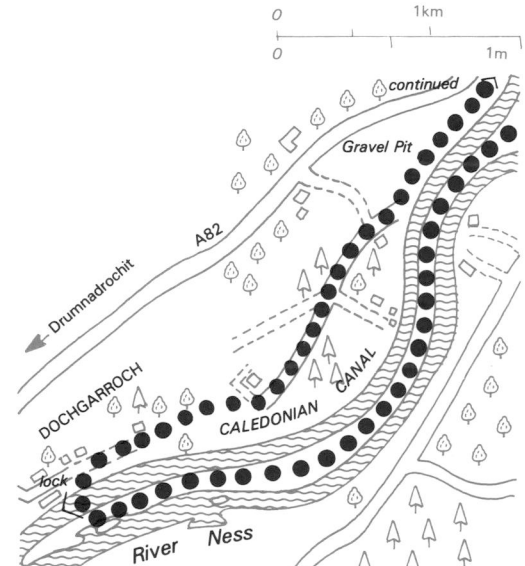

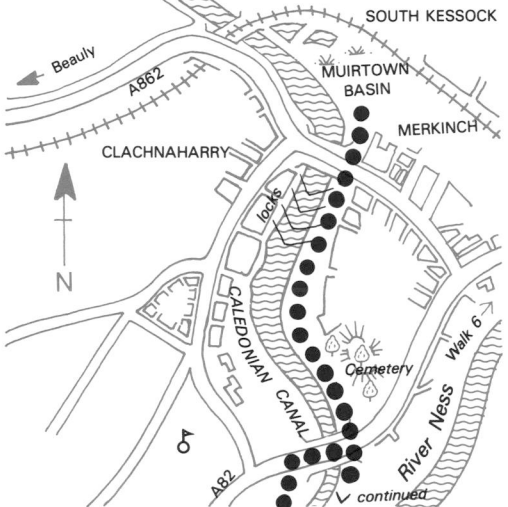

The Caledonian Canal was surveyed by Thomas Telford and built in the early 19th century, with the aim of eliminating the long and hazardous sea trip round the north coast of Scotland. It runs 60 miles (100km), from Inverness on the North Sea to Fort William on an arm of the Atlantic, following the line of the Great Glen: a natural furrow stretching from coast to coast along a fault line. 22 miles of this distance is covered by the canal; the balance through the lochs of Dochfour, Ness, Oich and Lochy. This route follows the canal from the Muirtown Basin to the last lock before Loch Ness, at Dochgarroch.

Muirtown Basin is the assembly point for ships waiting to pass through the swingbridge of the A862 and on into the canal. There are always boats to be seen here, tied to the wharf.

Across the road are the first four locks. The

canal has 28 altogether, lifting the ships to a height of 106ft (32m) above sea level at Loch Oich.

The path continues, past residential areas and the picturesque hill of the Tomnahuirich cemetery, to the bridge carrying the A82.

The road to the left here leads back into the centre of Inverness. The one directly opposite eventually joins up with the 'Inverness Islands' route *(6)*. For the longer route continue by the canal side. The path now runs along a narrow, wooded strip of land between the canal and the River Ness.

It is approximately 3½ miles (5.5km) from the A82 to Dochgarroch. The path back, along the north side, leaves the canal at the end of a small wood (see map), rejoining it 1½ miles (2.5km) further on and continuing to the A82 bridge.

8 Creag Phadrig

Length: 1 mile (1.5km)
Height climbed: 150ft (70m)
Grade: C
Public conveniences: Inverness
Public transport: Bus and train services to
Inverness from every direction

*A short hill walk through conifers to an
old hill fort. Very fine views and good
paths.*

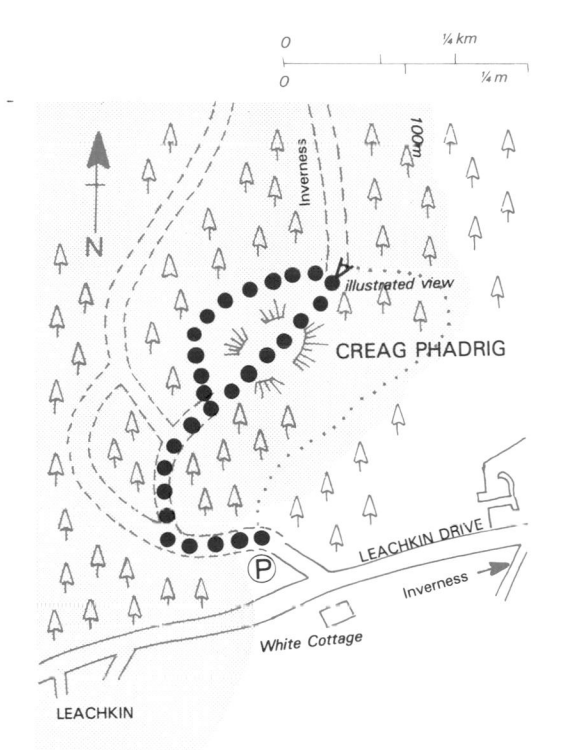

The fort on Creag Phadrig — its stone walls
fused by heat — was probably built over 2000
years ago. Very little of the structure — 260ft
(80m) long by 90ft (25m) wide — can now be
seen, except the grass mounds which have
grown over the walls, but it is a pleasant walk,
through a mature forest of spruce, fir, larch
and pine, and the views are excellent.

To reach the walk from Inverness, take the
Beauly road, over the Caledonian Canal, and
turn left up King Brude Road. Carry straight
on at the roundabout, up Leachkin Road.
Turn right on the road signposted to
Blackpark. The car park is on the right, just
opposite a white cottage — 2 miles (3km) from
the town centre.

The creag is in clear view, and the path to
the summit is well marked. Near the top it
becomes steep, but the going is never difficult.
The path approaches the fort from the west
and leaves it to the east, leading down to an
excellent viewpoint (see below) before cutting
round the hill to the left and rejoining the
original path.

An alternative return route is to follow the
path down the north slope; turning right at the
bottom to reach King Brude Road.

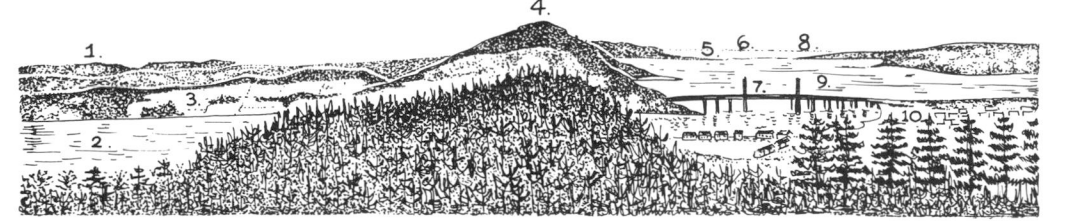

1. *Ben Wyvis* 2. *Beauly Firth* 3. *The Black Isle* 4. *Ord Hill* 5. *Chanonry Point* 6. *Moray Firth* 7. *Kessock Bridge*
8. *Fort George* 9. *Firth of Inverness* 10. *Inverness*

9 Reelig Glen

Length: 1½ miles (2.5km)
Height climbed: 200ft (60m)
Grade: C
Public conveniences: None
Public transport: None

A number of routes through mature mixed woodland, with particularly fine conifers. Paths good.

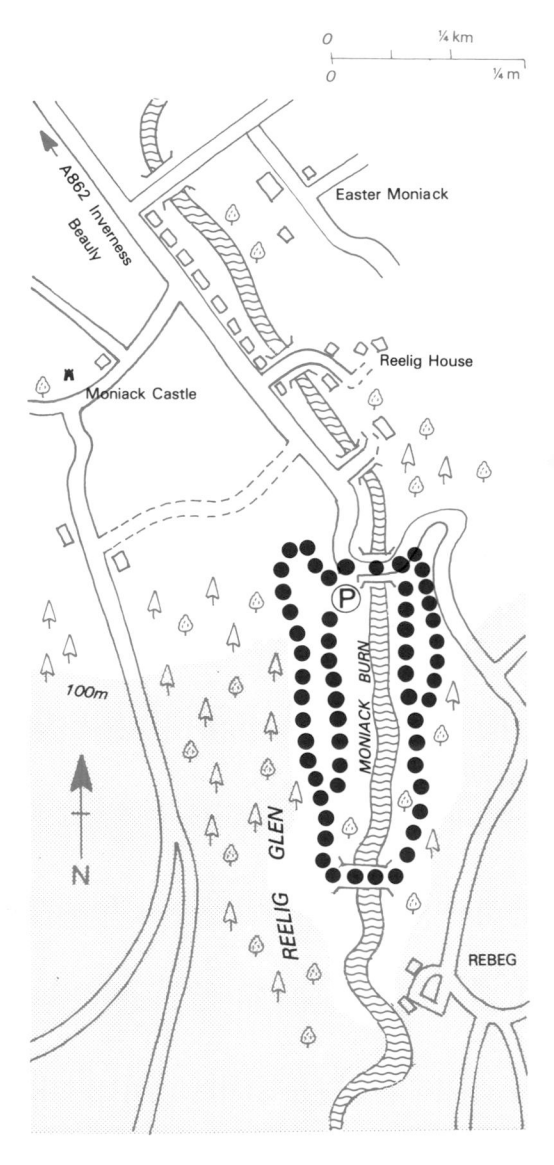

Reelig Glen lies some eight miles west of Inverness to the south of the A862 road to Beauly. Turn off this road and follow the signs for Moniack. Then, at the junction where Moniack Castle appears to the right, carry straight on, on the road signposted to Rebeg.

Reelig Glen was once — in common with so much of this corner of the country — the property of a branch of the Fraser family. It was sold to the Forestry Commission in 1949 for preservation and commercial development.

The glen was designed as a wooded, 'natural' garden, using many of the imported trees which are now associated with commercial forestry: Douglas fir, western red hemlock, Norway and Sitka spruce. The particular charm of this area is that the trees were planted so long ago (the glen was largely planned and planted by James Baillie Fraser, a writer and traveller, in the early 19th century) that they have attained a maturity which one rarely sees in Britain.

There are a number of paths through the glen, leading as far as a bridge over the burn, beside which are the ruins of a grotto — a common feature of planned gardens of the period. A leaflet is available from tourist and Forestry Commission offices which describes two particular routes, and provides a commentary on the points of interest along the way.

At one point, from the edge of the glen, there is a view across the surrounding countryside, including the Beauly Firth and Moniack Castle: a Fraser stronghold, now run as a winery.

10 Culburnie

Length: 5 miles (8km)
Height climbed: Negligible
Grade: B
Public conveniences: None
Public transport: None

An easy circuit on quiet, metalled, public roads, with views of the Beauly Firth and the surrounding farmland.

There is no particular reason why this road should be preferred to any other in the district. It is included as an example of one of the many pleasant minor roads in this low-lying V of land around the Beauly Firth, confined by the surrounding Highlands: from Inverness to Beauly — the Aird — and north-east into the Black Isle. This is an area of farmland and backroads and there are many walks to be found, with the aid of a detailed map.

To reach this route — from Inverness — take the A862 road towards Beauly, turning onto the A831 at the junction, and then taking the first turn to the left. There are no particular parking places, but a space can usually be found. Please remember to leave field entrances clear.

Start the route where you wish. The section from Hughton to Kiltarlity Cottage provides the best views, across the farmland to the Beauly Firth, and south to the hills above Loch Ness. Here the road is lined with dykes and oak trees.

Beyond the junction there are fine views of the steep river valley, and of the towers of Beaufort Castle, largely hidden by trees. The castle was built for Fraser of Lovat in 1880, the previous building on the site having been destroyed by the Duke of Cumberland in the aftermath of Culloden in 1746.

Beyond the castle the road continues through a mixture of farmland and woodland. Keep right at the turn off for Kiltarlity and straight on at the turn for Lonbuie to return to Hughton. Be adventurous though — the roads which radiate from this central circuit are all worth exploring. The route to Eskdale up the Beauly valley is particularly beautiful.

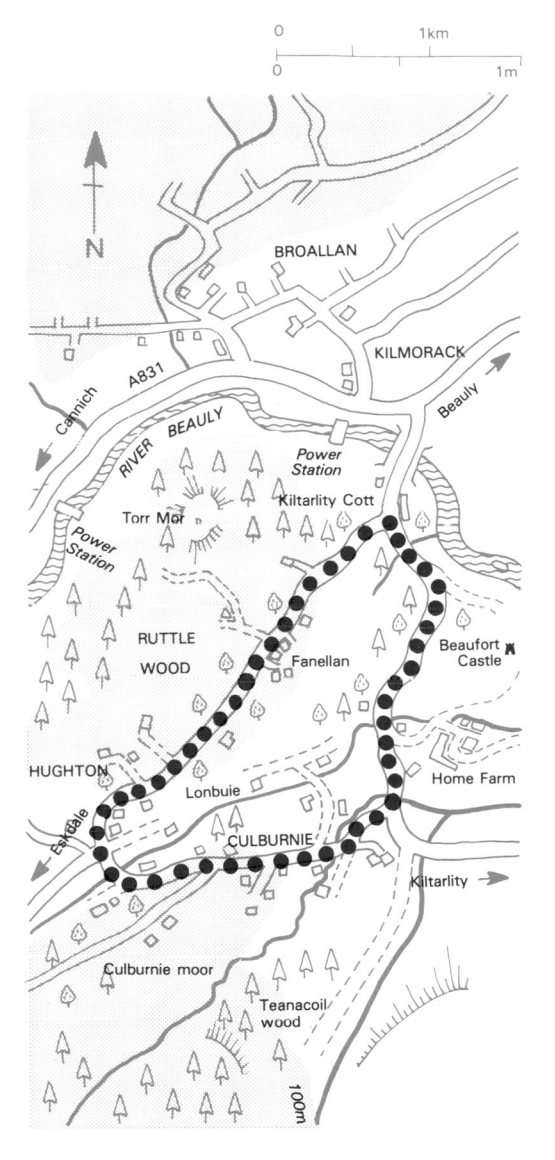

11 Dog Falls

Length: 4 miles (6.5km)
Height climbed: 350ft (100m)
Grade: B
Public conveniences: Car park
Public transport: None

A signposted trail through Scots pine forest, maintained in its natural state by the Forestry Commission. Path good.

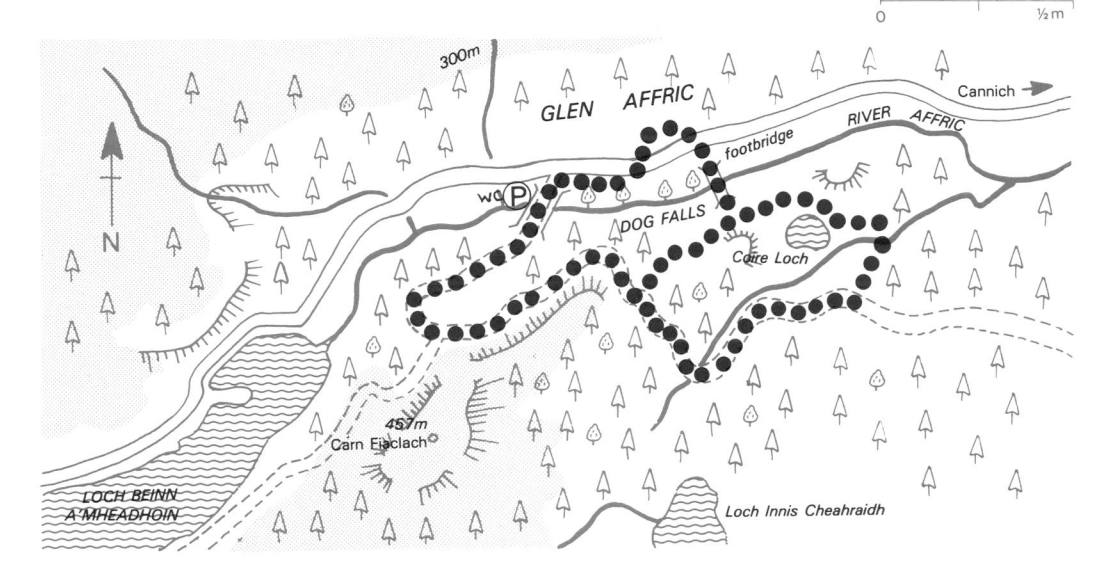

Due to climatic changes and excessive grazing and felling, the original Caledonian Pine Forest has been reduced to a few small pockets throughout the Highlands. Now, particularly around the Cairngorms *(25,30,32)* and here, in Glen Affric, efforts are being made to encourage the forest to regenerate naturally.

To reach Glen Affric from Inverness, take the A862 towards Beauly, turning on to the A831 for Cannich at the junction. Turn right at Cannich on the Glen Affric road. The car park for Dog Falls is about 4 miles (6.5km) up this road.

The walk, which is clearly signposted, leads across a bridge over the River Affric and up the hill. After a short climb the path reaches a point where the hill nudges out of its tree cover for a moment and there is a fine view of the glen, and of the peaks on the far side. The loch

below, to the left, is Loch Beinn a' Mheadhoin, which has been dammed for hydro-electricity.

A little further on the path splits. The shorter route cuts down to the left, and the longer continues to Coire Loch — a small, round, green lochan fringed with peat bogs and mosses and surrounded by the pines. Climb the rocky outcrop beyond the loch and then continue along the path, down to the stile and a second footbridge over the river, just below the falls.

The route crosses the road and continues through the regular ranks of commercial forestry, and then recrosses the road and returns to the car park.

The woods of Glen Affric are inhabited by one of Britain's rarest mammals — the pine marten. They are very reclusive, but there is always the chance of seeing one.

12 Loch Affric

Length: 10 miles (16km)
Height climbed: None
Grade: A
Public conveniences: None
Public transport: None

A long walk on rough paths and Forestry Commission tracks, across moorland between Loch Affric and the surrounding hills, scattered with stands of Scots pine.

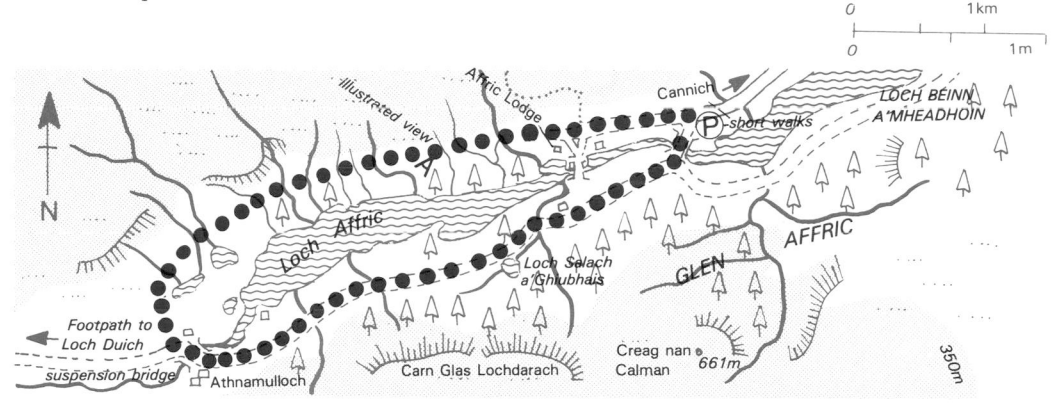

6 miles (9.5km) beyond the Dog Falls car park *(11)* the metalled road ends. There is a bridge here and a monument to the Clan Chisholm who once inhabited the glen. A forestry road continues for a further mile to the car park.

This is a lovely walk, between the steep hills and the loch, with the stands of pine by the water's edge. There is no difficulty with the route. On the north side of the loch it passes to the right of Affric Lodge, through a gate, and on across the moorland. The path is rough and damp, but clear enough.

At the west end of the loch the path splits. To the right is the start of the long footpath to Loch Duich in Kintail on the west coast. Keep left here, across a suspension bridge with a most exaggerated wiggle, past the cottage at Athnamulloch and across the floor of the glen to join the forestry track along the south side of the loch, back to the car park. Keep a look out for red deer along this route — particularly during the colder months.

There are two other short walks, along signposted routes, from the car park.

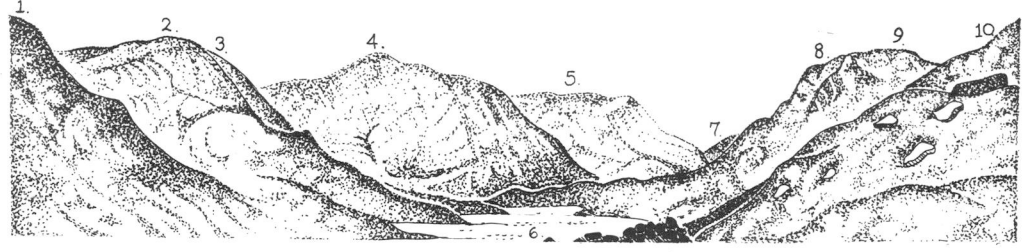

1. *Carn Glas Lochdaroch (771m)* 2. *Carn a' choire Ghairbh* 3. *Garbh Leac (1120m)*
4. *Mullach Fraoch-Choire (1102m)* 5. *Ciste Dubh (982m)* 6. *Loch Affric* 7. *Bienn Fhada (1032m)*
8. *Creag a' Chaorainn* 9. *Au Tudair* 10. *Sguur na Lapaich*

Walk 12

13 Plodda Falls

Length: 1½ miles (2.5km)
Height climbed: 200ft (60m)
Grade: C
Public conveniences: None
Public transport: None

A short walk through mature conifer forest to a spectacular waterfall. Paths good, but damp in places.

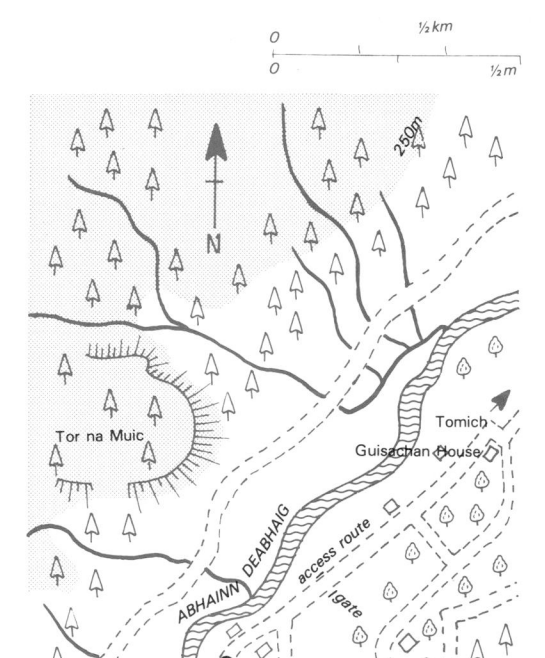

This short route is one for the afficionados of waterfalls. In a steep rocky gorge, overhung with vast conifers, the Eas Socach drops over 70ft (20m) into a pool swelled by the Abhainn Deabhag, which joins the burn of the falls at this point.

Quite half the fun of these falls is the difficulty of reaching them — not the walk (which is short, if steep) but the road to it.

The village of Cannich is in Strathglass, on the A831 between Drumnadrochit and Beauly. Just across the river from Cannich a small road branches off the A831, signposted to Tomich. Just beyond Tomich the road forks. There is no difficulty finding the falls — simply follow the signs — but drive slowly: the road suddenly degenerates into a track, riddled with potholes.

After about a mile the track goes through a gate (please remember to close this), beyond which are the ruins of Guisachan House, set in a broad parkland scattered with large trees. The ruins are in a dangerous condition and should not be entered.

At the far end of the park there is another gate and, a little further on, a car park.

The path sets off by the side of the river, and climbs to the edge of the gorge, giving a distant view of the fall. There are two further views: one from the edge of the bowl, in the spray at the foot of the fall; the other from a bridge directly above it.

Follow the path back down from this bridge and turn right, towards a stand of vast conifers, towering like cathedral pillars above the mossy forest floor.

Turn left at the road to return to the car park.

14 Fort Augustus to Glen Moriston

Length: 7 miles (11km) one way
Height climbed: 1200ft (360m)
Grade: A
Public conveniences: Fort Augustus
Public transport: Bus services from Inverness
stopping at Invermoriston and Fort Augustus

*A steep hill crossing, through forestry and
across moorland, on an old military road.
Very damp, and some athleticism is
required when crossing burns.*

The military roads of the Highlands were built
by the Hanoverians in the 18th century as part
of the effort to curb the power of the Jacobite
clans. Large stretches are now incorporated
into the main road network; other sections —
particularly the high hill passes, unsuitable for
cars — remain as they were.

The route between Fort Augustus and Glen
Moriston was part of a road — engineered in
1755, but widely used before that by cattle
drovers and the military — to Skye.

This section starts at Jenkins Park. Follow
the road signs from the north end of Fort
Augustus. The road splits, with a group of
white houses on the right hand side of the right
fork. Park opposite these.

Beyond the houses a forestry track goes
through a gate — follow this. A short way
beyond the gate the route to Glen Moriston is
signposted to the right.

The path zig-zags up the hill — at the top of
which there are excellent views of Fort Augustus,
Loch Ness, Loch Oich, the Caledonian Canal
and the Monadhliath Mountains beyond the
Great Glen. It then plunges into dense forestry.
Two miles further on the road emerges onto
the moor. The path is very clear at this point,
but disappears as it approaches Allt
Phocaichain. Its restart on the opposite side of
the glen is quite visible. There is no bridge over
the burn, which is quite large and, in spate,
may need to be forded rather than jumped.

Beyond the burn the track is quite clear,
leading across the moor, down to the edge of
the forest, and then cutting through the trees
to the Glen Moriston Road. This final section
includes some of the original bridges; the
largest over Allt a'Chaise.

15 Inchnacardoch Forest

Length: 3½ miles (5.5km)
Height climbed: None
Grade: C
Public conveniences: None
Public transport: Bus service between Inverness and Fort William; stopping at Fort Augustus

A forest walk through dense, commercial conifer forestry, including a path along the River Oich. Paths good, but damp beside the river.

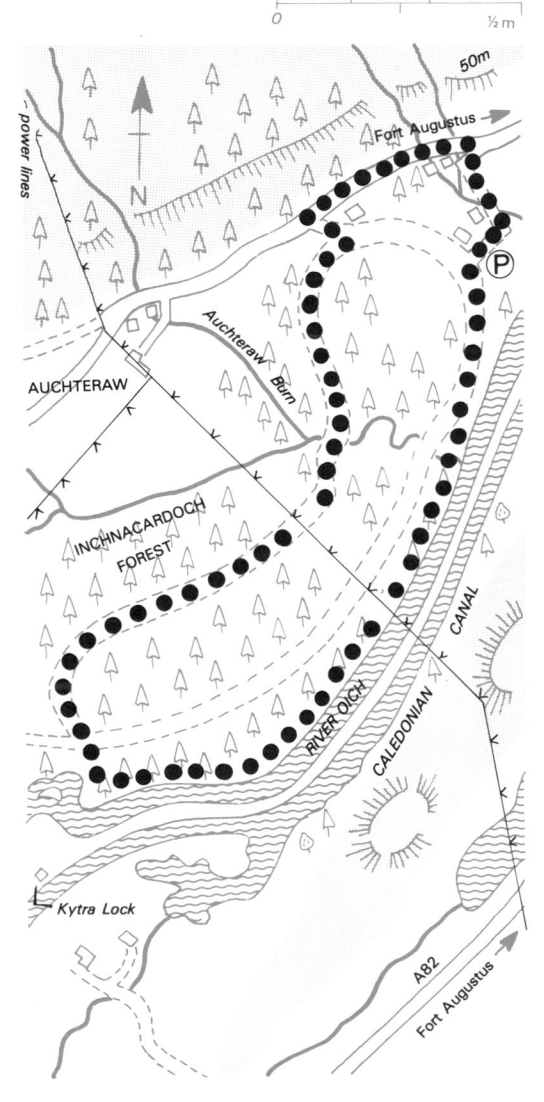

This route is not unlike every other walk through commercial forestry in the area, but it is considerably lifted by a charming section along the banks of the River Oich, where the river runs in close parallel to the Caledonian Canal.

To reach the route turn left off the A82 Inverness to Fort Augustus road, just north of Fort Augustus, on the road signposted to Auchteraw. The car park is on the left, 1 mile (1.5km) along this road.

The route starts at the back of the car park and joins the river bank soon after crossing Auchteraw burn. The canal — which runs between Inverness and Fort William — is beyond the river, across a narrow partition.

Just after passing a small wooded island, at a bend in the river, the path cuts into the forest and heads back towards the car park. After recrossing the burn it veers left, eventually joining the public road. Walk a short way along this to return to the car park.

At the end of the Auchteraw road there is another car park and further walks through the forest.

16 Foyers to Whitebridge

Length: 6 miles (9.5km) there and back
Height climbed: Negligible
Grade: B
Public conveniences: Upper Foyers
Public transport: Bus service between Inverness and Foyers

A pleasant walk through forests and farmland by the side of the River Foyers, including a detour to the dramatic Falls of Foyers. Paths of uneven quality.

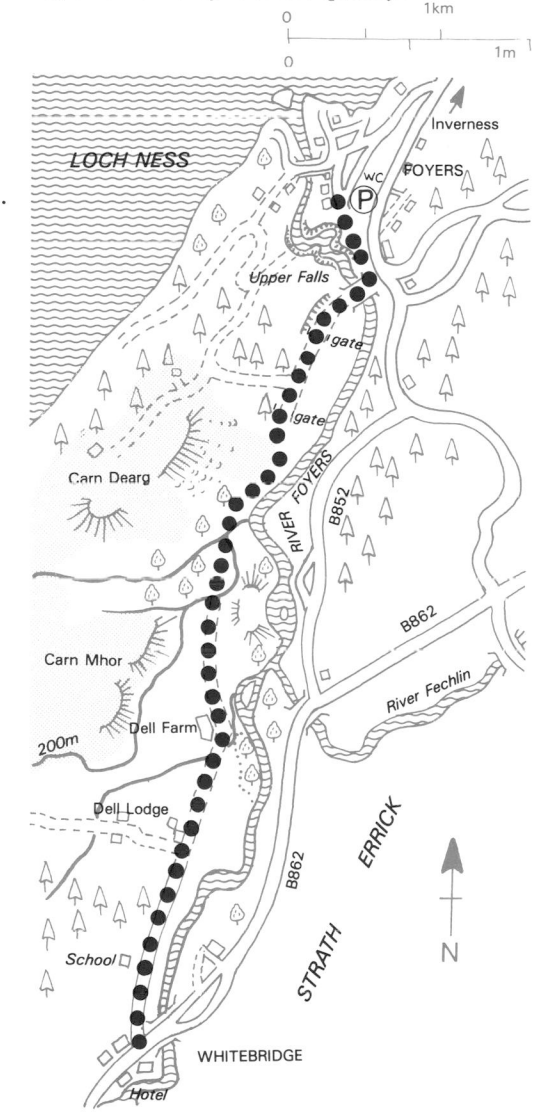

The River Foyers originates in the high moors of the Monadhliath Mountains, to the south, and meanders slowly through the flat land of Strath Errick before falling 450ft (130m) in under a mile, from the upper falls to Loch Ness.

Take the B862 from Inverness to Dores, and then the B852 to Foyers. Park just beyond the shop. There are a great many paths through the conifer woods around the deep gorge and falls of the river. A potential use for these falls was spotted in 1896, when a hydro-electric power station — one of the earliest in Britain — was built to power the local aluminium works, which at one time produced one sixth of the total world aluminium production.

The route to Whitebridge starts a little further along the B852, where a path cuts off to the right, across the river. This path continues under the side of a wooded cliff before disappearing into a stand of conifers. Beyond the plantation there is a field. Cross this, bearing to the left of the wooded hill, towards the river. Pass through the wood and, at the far end, cross the burn and head for a gap between two hills. The path is clear from here on, past the farm at Dell and on, down the metalled road to Whitebridge.

The countryside around this walk is typical of the strange, lumpy, contorted landscape between the Monadhliaths and Loch Ness; punctuated with abrupt hills and cliffs and scattered with small lochs.

Whitebridge was a staging point on General Wade's military road between Inverness and Fort Augustus and, beside the modern road bridge, the original — built over the River Foyers in 1733 — is still standing.

Either return by the same route or double back along the B862 and the B852.

17 Farigaig Forest

Length: Up to 2 miles (3km), plus extensions
Height climbed: 350ft (100m)
Grade: C
Public conveniences: Car park
Public transport: Bus service between Inverness and Foyers

A selection of easy routes, of different lengths, through broad-leaved and coniferous woodland, with extensions on quiet country roads.

The hills on the south side of Loch Ness present a steep, unbroken curtain, dropping to the water's edge. Such burns and rivers as penetrate this curtain do so with a mixture of steep gorges and waterfalls. Such a gorge ends at Inverfarigaig, in a garden of natural and landscaped woodland.

From Inverness, take the B862 to Dores, and then the B852 along the lochside. Turn left at the sign for Farigaig Forest Centre.

Beside the car park there is an exhibition centre covering the evolution of the surrounding countryside. In addition there is a leaflet which provides a commentary on points of interest along the paths, and outlines the four available routes, which pass through the broad-leaved woodland of the narrow pass of Inverfarigaig, and the coniferous forestry of the hill to the south of the pass. Among the conifers there are Norway and Sitka spruce, Douglas fir, larch and red cedar — some of which have grown to a considerable height and girth — while the broad-leaved woodland includes birch, alder, oak, ash and others.

Along the routes there are views across Loch Ness to the north, and east to the Monadhliath Mountains.

One possible extension to these paths is to continue beyond Lochan Torr a Tuill and return along the public road (see map). Another alternative is to walk down to the B852 and turn right, across the River Farigaig, and then right again, up an unsignposted road. This road zig-zags to the top of the ridge and gives splendid views of the Pass of Inverfarigaig, and south, across Loch Ness.

Route 1	*River Trail*
Route 2	*Road Trail*
Route 3	*Glenlia Trail*
Route 4	*Stockade Trail*

18 Loch Duntelchaig

Length: 5½ miles (9km)
Height climbed: 200ft (50m)
Grade: B
Public conveniences: None
Public transport: None

A high walk along metalled roads and a rough footpath; by the banks of two lochs; through forestry, woodland and the open moor.

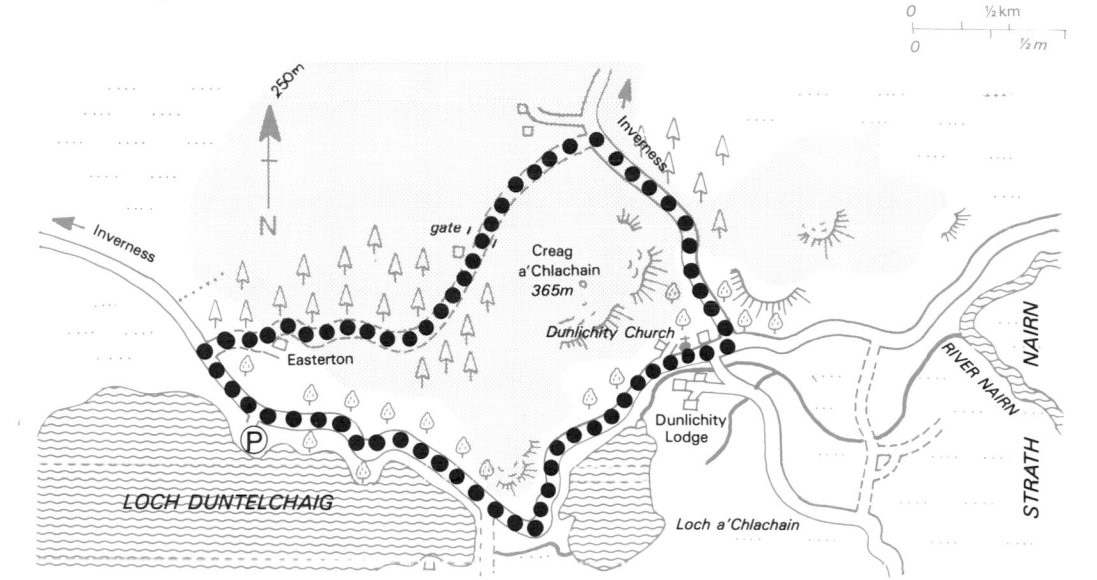

This route should be of particular interest to anyone of the surname MacGillivray, for upper Strath Nairn was the family homeland, and the church at Dunlichity the burial ground of the chiefs of the clan.

The loch can be difficult to find, but a road map should show an unnumbered road, following the route of an old military road from Inverness to Loch Ashie. Turn left at the junction here for Loch Duntelchaig.

Starting from the parking place by the lochside walk a short way back along the road and turn right, up the road to Easterton. Keep to the left of the farm and continue over the hill. This part of the route is quite rugged and can be wet. The land to either side is planted with conifers. Turn right at the end of the track and walk down the road towards Dunlichity through mixed woodland, with the rugged

Creag a' Chlachain to the right. Turn right at the junction.

The church is on a mediaeval religious site. This church was rebuilt in the 18th and 19th centuries. The gatehouse, built in 1820, is quite charming, but it had a rather unpleasant purpose — a guard was stationed here to prevent grave robberies. Beside the MacGillivrays lie many others of related clans: Mackintoshes, MacBains, Shaws and MacPhersons.

The road now continues along the edge of little Loch a'Chlachain before cutting right, up the short connecting glen, and skirting the shores of Loch Duntelchaig through a wood of birch and rowan.

To the left at this point is the rocky bulk of Stac na Cathaig (*Hill of the Jackdaws*); typical of the abrupt hills which punctuate the strange and distinctive landscape of the area.

19 Strath Dearn

Length: 6 miles (9.5km) to Dalarossie and back
Height climbed: Negligible
Grade: B
Public conveniences: None
Public transport: None

A pleasant walk along a metalled public road, through a wide, steep-sided Highland glen with a variety of farmland and woodland.

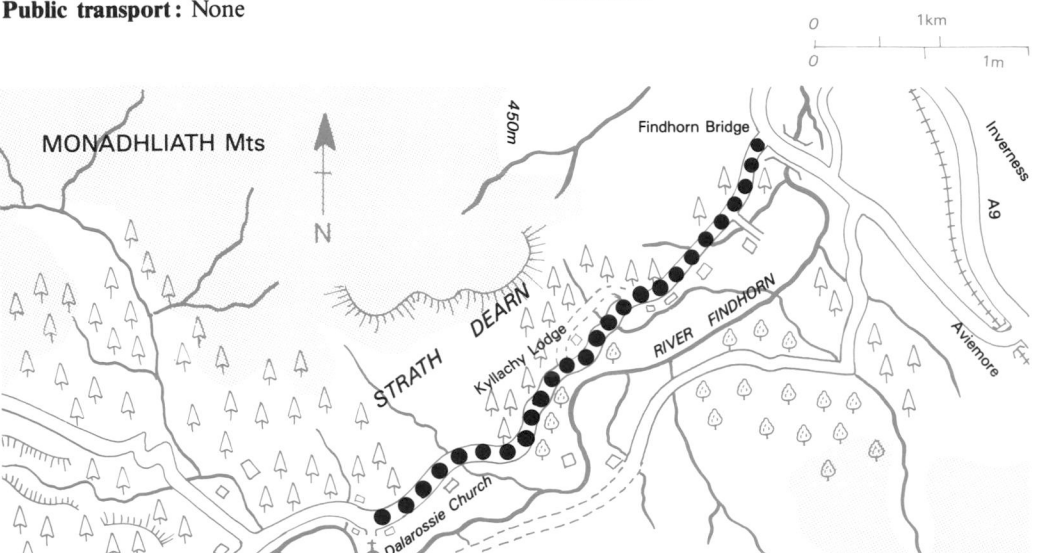

Strath Dearn is the upper glen of the River Findhorn, where it winds itself into the heart of the massif of the Monadhliath Mountains. The river flows some 50 miles (80km) from the bleak hills north of Laggan to its tidal basin amongst the sand dunes and farmlands of Moray. The Findhorn is a good salmon river and some of these fascinating fish may be seen skimming through the shallow waters, on their way to the head waters of the river to spawn.

To reach Strath Dearn turn off the A9 road — between Inverness and Perth — at the sign for Tomatin, some 16 miles (26km) south of Inverness, and turn left at the first junction. Follow this road through Tomatin and on to Findhorn Bridge. There are no particular parking places, so please be careful not to block any entrances.

Start walking up the road signposted to Coignafearn. The floor of the strath is a flat alluvial plain, typical of the glaciated valleys of the area. It is fertile and supports a mixture of crops and animals. The surrounding hills are steep, and become more so as the road continues up the valley. There is a mixture of natural broad-leaved and coniferous woodland throughout the glen.

About 3 miles (5km) from Findhorn Bridge is Dalarossie Church — a small building, built in 1790 on an older religious site. The church has a lovely position, in a field in a crook of the river.

Turn here or walk further up the glen. Return by the same route.

20 Brodie Castle

Length: 2 miles (3km)
Height climbed: None
Grade: C
Public conveniences: Car park
Public transport: Bus service between Inverness
and Forres

*A short walk through farmland and
woodland along clear paths and quiet
country roads; through the grounds of
Brodie Castle — open to the public.*

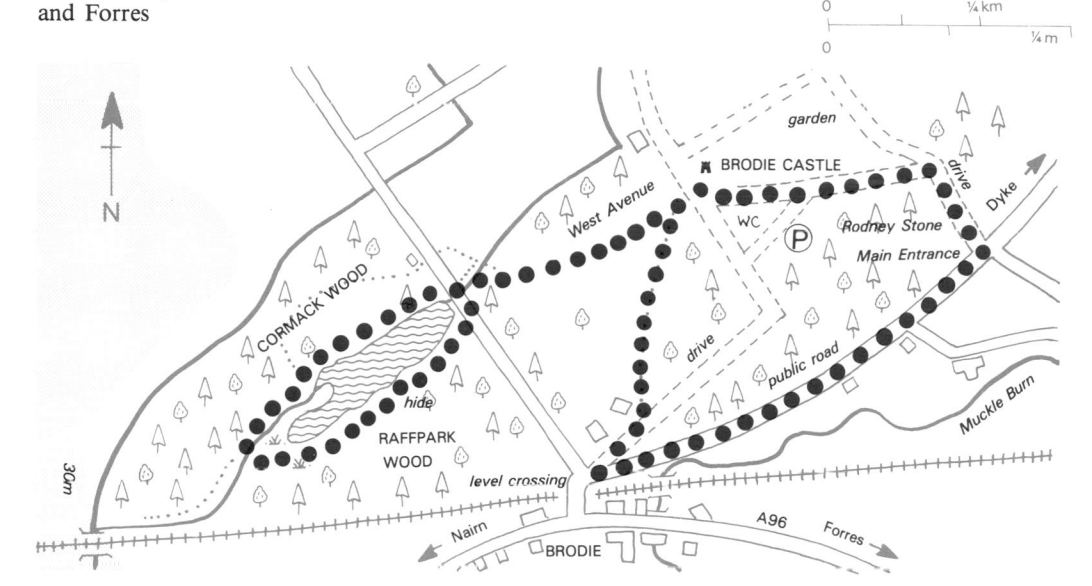

The Brodie family have been living on this spot
since before records were begun. The first
mention is made in 1249, and a romantic, and
not improbable theory traces the family name
back to 'Brude' — a common name amongst
the Pictish kings who used Inverness as a
centre. The present castle was begun in the mid
16th century and has been added to at various
times since then. It is open to the public during
the summer. The castle is signposted from the
A96 Inverness to Aberdeen road, 6 miles
(9.5km) east of Nairn.

There are a number of paths through the
castle grounds and gardens, which are notable
for their great number and variety of daffodils.
For this route, walk west from the castle along
the West Avenue — lined with a great variety
of trees, principally copper beech and lime. Cut
off the main path and cross the public road.

The shallow pond beyond is entirely man made,
and both it and the stream which feeds it are
cobbled. The bird life here — which includes
heron, coot and even the occasional visiting
osprey — can be viewed from a hide on the
south side of the pond.

After circling the pond recross the road and
follow the path back down West Avenue,
turning right before reaching the castle, down
the path to Brodie village. Walk out of the
castle grounds, turn left and walk along the
quiet public road to the main entrance, and
then up the driveway. A short distance from
the gate, up the drive, is the Rodney Stone — a
9th century Pictish symbol stone with abstract
symbols on one side and a Christian cross on
the other.

The drive now continues to the car park,
and then on to the castle.

21 Monaughty Forest

Length: 3 miles (5km) of pathways; various routes
Height climbed: 150ft (50m)
Grade: C
Public conveniences: None
Public transport: None

A series of signposted forest walks through commercial coniferous woodland. Paths good.

Route 1   *Red Route*
Route 2   *Green Route*
Route 3   *Blue Route*

Behind Elgin the land begins to slope gently upwards: these are the most northerly foothills of the central Grampain range. In this low hill country there is considerable forestry. Monaughty Forest sits on Heldon Hill, over-looking Pluscarden Priory in the glen of the Black Burn to the south, and the flat lands towards the Moray Firth to the north. The forest walks are on the low, northern edge of the hill.

To reach Monaughty Forest from Elgin take the B9010 road (a back road to Forres) and cut right on to an unnumbered road 1 mile

(1.5km) after crossing the railway line. The car park is 3 miles (5km) along this road.

There are three walks of various lengths signposted here, giving good views to the east and south, and an excellent one, from the Blue route, towards the Moray Firth.

The forest is largely of commercial conifers at various stages of development — from recent planting to felling — with interspersed broad-leaved woodland.

22 Moray Coast

Length: Up to 20 miles (32km)
Height climbed: None
Grade: A/B/C
Public conveniences: Findhorn Dunes, Roseisle Forest and large towns
Public transport: Check locally

The Moray coast combines splendid sandy beaches with steep cliffs and stacks. A number of useful access points to the shoreline are listed below.

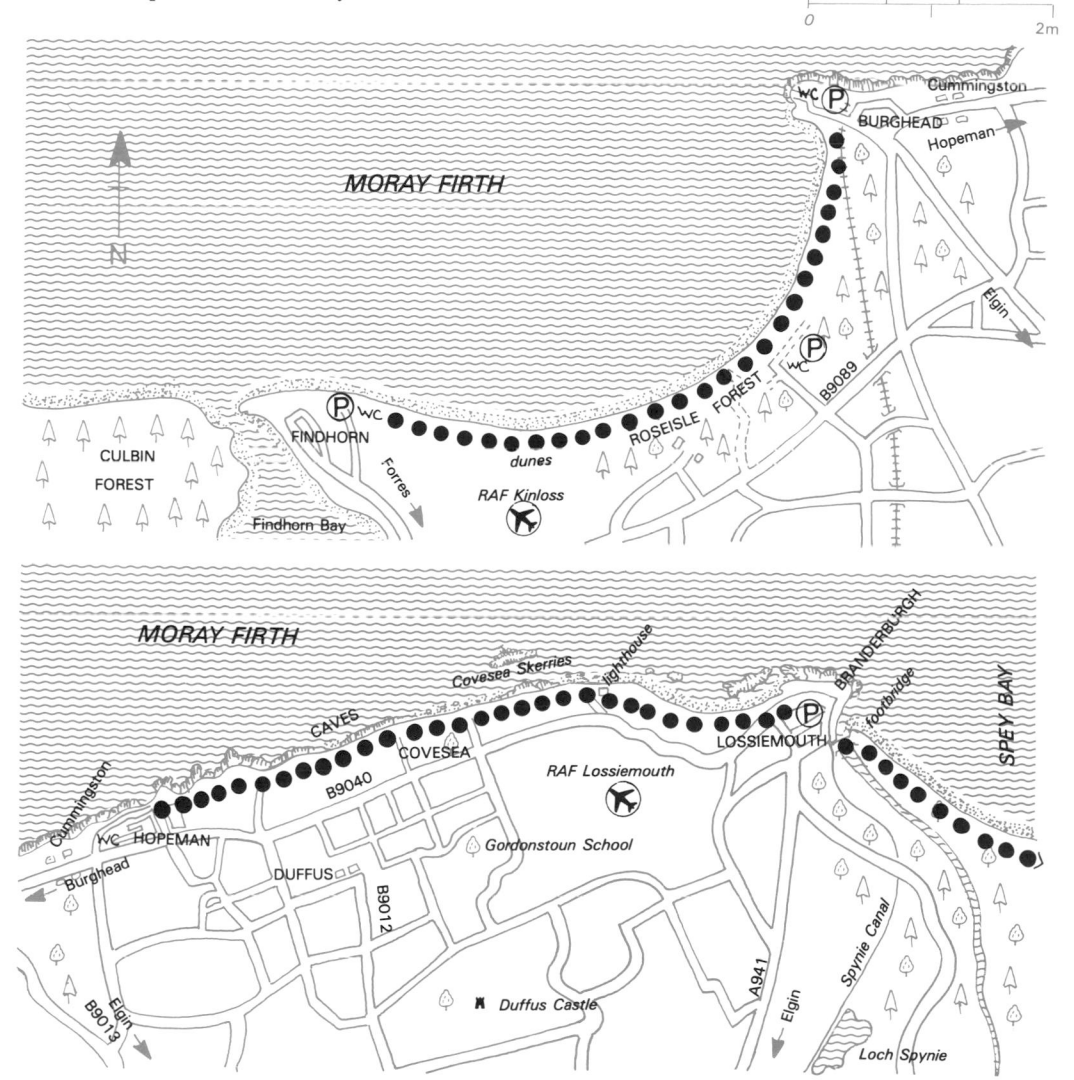

The distinctive wedge shaped Moray Firth, which chips into the north east corner of Scotland, takes its name from the old county of Moray (from the Gaelic Moireabh — *Sea Settlement*) on its southern shore. The Laich (or 'lower part') of Moray provides a low hinterland to the shoreline, largely formed of deposits from the retreating glaciers of the last ice age, 10,000 years ago. This light soil, though fertile, has proved to be a mixed blessing over the years. After the Rivers Nairn, Findhorn, Lossie and Spey have carried it down to the firth it is swiftly swept ashore again as sand. From the village of Findhorn at the mouth of Findhorn Bay — a broad tidal estuary — the edge of the vast Culbin forest can be seen, which was planted to stabilise the dunes of the Culbin sands which, in 1694, had engulfed the village and mansion of Culbin. A similar fate befell the original village of Findhorn, while the town built to replace it was destroyed by flood in 1701. The present village of Findhorn — which is very charming — has avoided all such disasters to date.

From Findhorn there is an excellent beach of golden sand as far as Burghead. The beach is backed, as far as the forest (see map), by a wide area of dunes and marram grass. Beyond the dunes is RAF Kinloss.

In the forest itself there is a car park and picnic site at Roseisle.

Findhorn — although it was once an important port — is now largely a recreational area. Burghead, on the other hand, is a fishing port. It is not old, dating back only to the early 19th century when it was used as a port for shipping out the vast amounts of grain produced in the Laich.

The shoreline to the east of Burghead is of a different character to that to the west, being tough and rocky. 1½ miles (2km) to the east of Burghead is Hopeman: another relatively modern village, founded by William Young of Burghead in 1805. From here there is a good walk to Lossiemouth. The coast is very rocky with cliffs, quarries and caves as far as Covesea. One of these caves is known as the 'Laird's Stable', and is thought to have been utilised for this purpose by Sir Robert Gordon, hiding his horses from both armies during the 1745 Jacobite rising.

The shifting sands had a large part in the creation of the next town along the coast: Lossiemouth. As late as the 15th century the port for the important city of Elgin was 4 miles (6.5km) inland at Spynie, which at that time stood at the head of a broad estuary. However, the sands shifted and blocked the mouth of the estuary, which became a shallow inland loch some 5 miles (8km) in length. The loch was eventually drained in 1860 and a canal was built from Spynie to the coast, but it became unworkable due to storm damage. In the meantime a new port had been built at the mouth of the River Lossie: Lossiemouth.

Through the years Lossiemouth has been an important and innovative fishing port. In 1879 William Campbell, a local skipper, designed and built the first of the giant 'Zulu' type lug-rigged ketches, which became such a feature of the east coast herring fishery. At the height of the herring boom up to 700 Scottish boats, some up to 80ft (25m) in length, would make the annual trip south, chasing the herring to the East Anglian ports.

A more modern development at Lossiemouth is the RAF base, to the west of the town.

There is a footbridge across the river here, and many miles of clear sandy beach to the east of the river, towards the mouth of the River Spey.

All along this coast there are splendid views across the firth to the hills of Cromarty, Sutherland and Caithness.

23 Speyside Way

Length: Up to 30 miles (48km)
Height climbed: 500ft (150m) over the length of the way
Grade: A/B/C
Public conveniences: Major towns along the way
Public transport: Check locally

A long distance footpath by the River Spey. This can be joined at a number of places along the route, some of which are listed below.

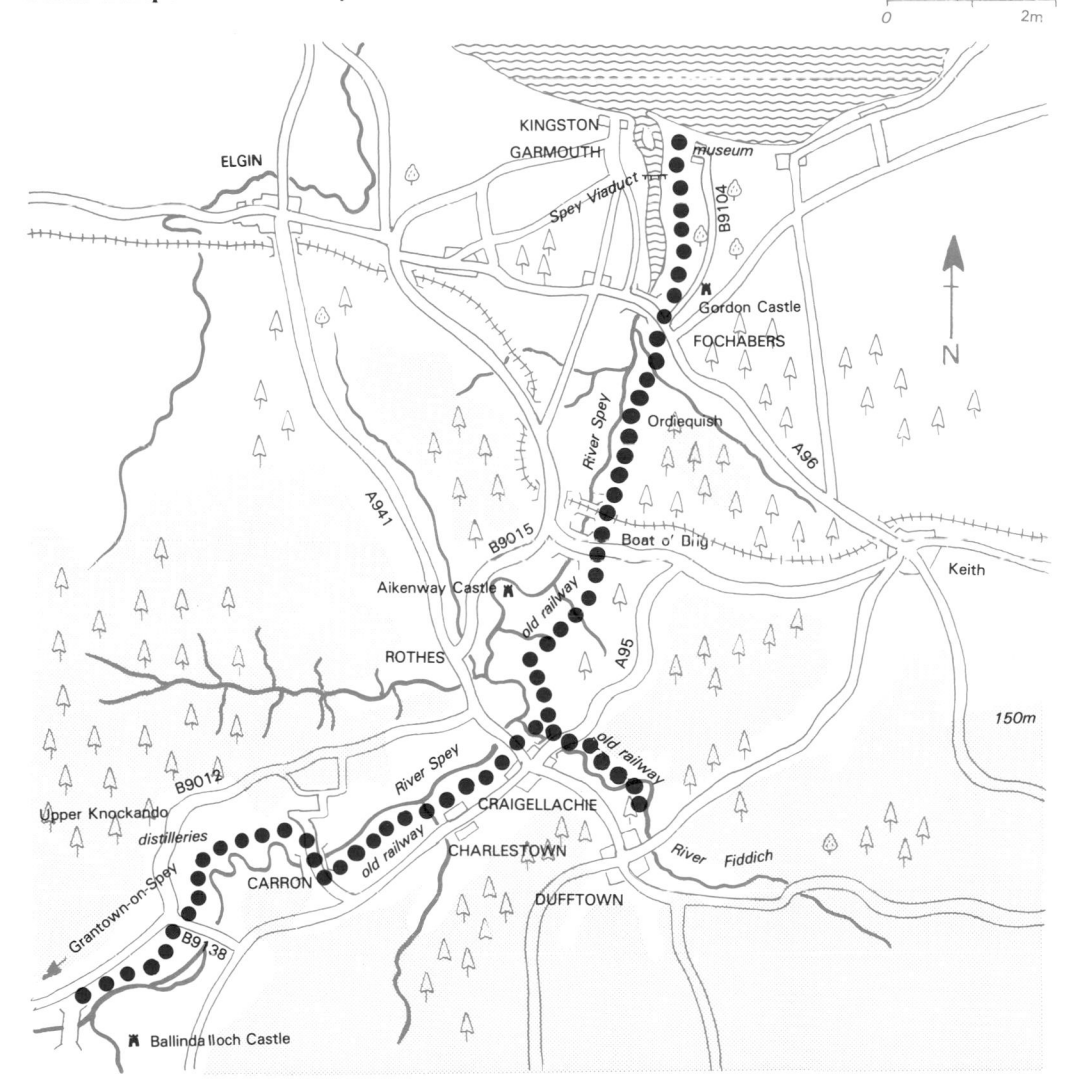

The Spey is the second longest river in Scotland, flowing 98 miles (145km) from the Monadhliath Mountains to Spey Bay on the Moray Firth. Virtually the whole length of the river is included within the area covered by this book and a number of routes run beside it or in view of it. The walks around Glenmore and the Cairngorms cross its tributaries. The river has no estuary and is too swift and shallow to be navigable, but it is a useful river — its waters are used extensively in the production of malt whisky, and it is one of the finest of Scotland's salmon rivers.

In recent years a footpath has been started, which it is intended should eventually run from Spey Bay to Glenmore. The first half of this footpath has been completed — from Spey Bay to Ballindalloch. This path covers approximately 30 miles (48km) in all, and can be joined and left at a number of places.

The last few miles of the Spey's progress are across flat farmland. The river does not meander but it widens and becomes split by a bewildering number of shifting shoals and islands. Indeed, the river and the tides of the firth act with such force upon the seashore that three times this century it has been necessary to re-cut the mouth of the river to prevent flooding.

In the 19th century the village of Kingston was the foremost shipbuilding centre in the north of Scotland, using wood floated down the Spey from as far as Glenmore. However, the forests became exhausted and shipbuilding changed from wood and wind to steam and steel, and before long the industry disappeared from the river.

Garmouth — joined to the Speyside Way by a footpath over the disused railway viaduct — was once a considerable port, but the river shifted and left the town too far from the water.

Salmon fishing has been carried out at Speymouth continuously for many centuries, although the level of netting is now restricted. There is a small museum of the industry at Spey Bay, inside an old ice house. This half-buried building, built in 1830, was used until recently to keep the fish fresh until they could be transported to the markets.

The Speyside Way follows quiet tracks up the east side of the river for the 4 miles (6.5km) to Fochabers — a town laid out at the end of the 18th century by John Baxter, for the 4th Duke of Gordon — and continues from the east end of the town along the Ordiequish road, 6 miles (9.5km) to Boat o'Brig.

The next section, to Craigellachie, is 7 miles (11km) in length. It starts along forestry tracks through a forest of commercial conifers, and then joins a quiet public road for the last three miles. Whisky drinkers should now start to recognise many of the names on a detailed map: the path crosses Glen Fiddich (for instance) just before the end of the section. Craigellachie also has a distillery, and a fine iron bridge over the Spey, designed by Thomas Telford.

At Craigellachie the route splits — both tracks following the course of the disused railway line. To the south-east it travels 5 miles (8km) to Dufftown; while, to the south-west, it follows the line through Charleston of Aberlour and past the distilleries at Carron, Knockando and Tamdhu. The route ends at the station yard at Ballindalloch. The last section is 12 miles (19km) in length.

The Speyside Way is too long and too diverse to describe in detail, but any section of it is worth investigating. A number of leaflets have been published by the Moray District Council, describing points of interest on each section.

24 Millbuies

Length: 2 miles (3km)
Height climbed: Negligible
Grade: C
Public conveniences: Car park
Public transport: Bus service from Elgin

A number of paths through a wooded public park laid out around a small loch. Paths good.

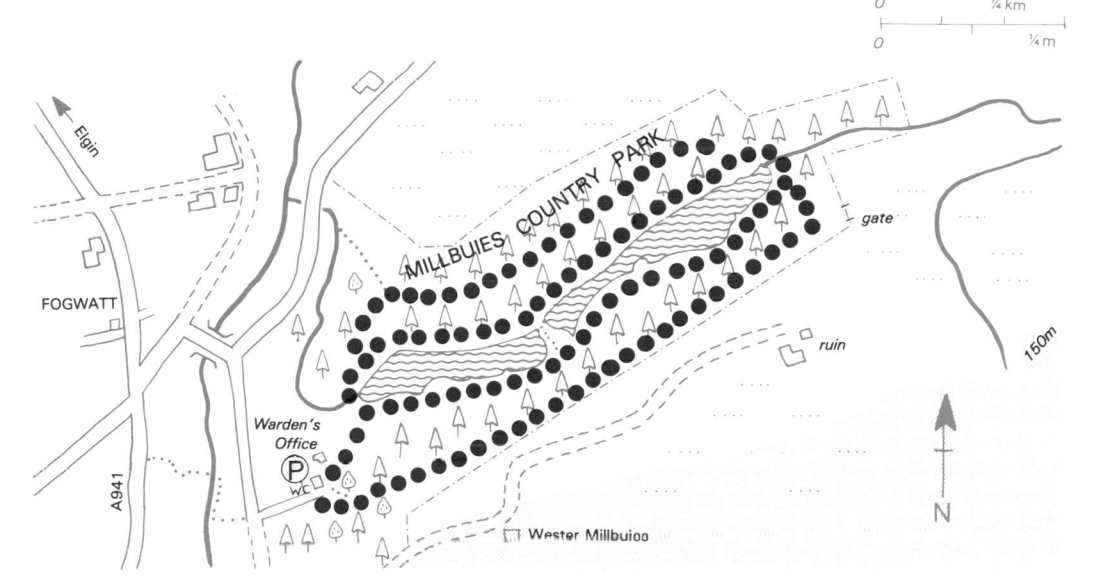

The Millbuies Loch was formed at the turn of the century when the landowners dammed the Millbuies Burn, to provide angling facilities. The surrounding land was improved by subsequent owners until, in 1956, it was gifted to the Elgin Town Council.

It consists of a shallow loch surrounded by low, wooded hills. The loch is stocked and daily fly fishing permits are available.

To reach Millbuies take the A941 from Elgin towards Perth, and turn off the road at Fogwatt. The park is signposted.

In the car park there is an information board, and leaflets describing the 'tree trail' and 'plant trail' are available from the warden's office. These are not essential to the enjoyment of the place, but they do give an idea of the variety of flora to be found here. The tree

guide lists 17 species — each one named and numbered along the way. There are over 30 varieties of rhododendrons.

For a general walk around the park, start along the faint path leading up the bank to the right of the car park, through a wood of pine and larch. Turn left at the top, with the farmland over the fence to the right of the path. From this stretch of the path there are good views of the Moray Firth.

At the end of the wood there is a gate in the fence. Stay this side of it and turn left, down some steps to the head of the loch. From here there are three different routes back to the car park: down either side of the loch, or through the conifers on the opposite bank, on the other side of the loch.

25 Loch Garten

Length: 2 miles (3km)
Height climbed: None
Grade: C
Public conveniences: None
Public transport: None

A short, pleasant track through the Scots pine woodland of the RSPB nature reserve, famous for its Ospreys. Path good.

Loch Garten is known to most people through its association with ospreys. These birds had not been seen in Scotland since the early part of the 20th century until a pair nested at Loch Garten in 1959, and their numbers throughout the Highlands have been increasing ever since. There is a hide above Loch Garten from which the nesting birds can be viewed.

To reach the walk, turn into Boat of Garten off the A95 between Aviemore and Grantown-on-Spey. Cross the bridge over the River Spey and turn left at the junction on to the B970. Take the first turn to the right. The car park is 1 mile (1.5km) along this road, on the right.

The path is very clear: forking soon after it reaches Loch Garten. It makes no difference which fork is taken as the path runs in a loop, up to the edge of Loch Mallachie.

The wood is semi-natural Scots pine — many of the trees are very old, while others have been planted recently.This type of woodland encourages the specialist bird life — in particular the crested tit, Scottish crossbill and capercaillie, which — in this country — only breed in the conifer forests of the Highlands. Watch also for water fowl on the lochs.

26 Boat of Garten

Length: 2 miles (3km)
Height climbed: None
Grade: C
Public conveniences: Boat of Garten
Public transport: Bus service between Aviemore and Grantown-on-Spey

A short walk along the banks of the River Spey, through fields and mixed woodland. The path is likely to be wet in places and there are a number of stiles to be crossed.

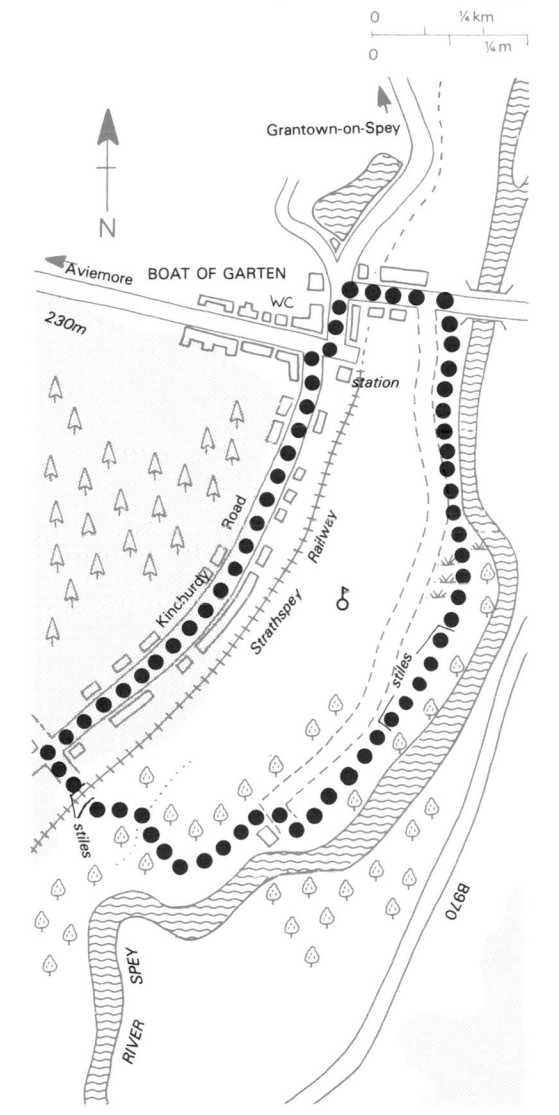

The Spey is the second longest river in Scotland, and Boat of Garten is about midway along its course: approximately (ignoring the more extreme wiggles) 40 miles (65km) south of its mouth at Spey Bay and 45 miles (70km) north of its source at Loch Spey. Already, fed by the hill burns of the Monadhliaths and the Cairngorms, the river is broad and fast flowing. This route follows a short stretch of the river.

Boat of Garten is 5 miles (8km) north of Aviemore, just off the A95 road to Grantown-on-Spey. Park in the town and walk down to the bridge over the river. The town is named after the ferry which used to cross the river at this point. Just before the bridge there is a sign to the right of the road, indicating the 'Riverside Walk'.

The path follows the very edge of the river and can be very damp. In addition there are a number of stiles to be negotiated along the way, but it is a pleasant walk, initially through mixed broad-leaved woodland and then through fields. Watch out for water fowl on the river.

When the path reaches the white house at Wester Dalvoult turn right, just before the house, and follow the path to a junction at the foot of a steep slope. Turn left here. The path skirts around the hill and turns to the right, into a pleasant area of mixed woodland. Carry straight on, crossing the railway line. This is the Strathspey Railway: a steam line running between Aviemore and Boat of Garten.

Beyond the railway the path cuts through a wood of Scots pine before joining Kinchurdy Road. Turn right here, along a metalled road, to return to the town.

27 Sluggan Pass

Length: 6 miles (9.5km) there and back
Height climbed: 450ft (130m)
Grade: B
Public conveniences: Glenmore
Public transport: Bus service between Aviemore and the ski slopes; stops at Glenmore

A forest walk on good roads leading to a steep-sided pass, with possible extensions.

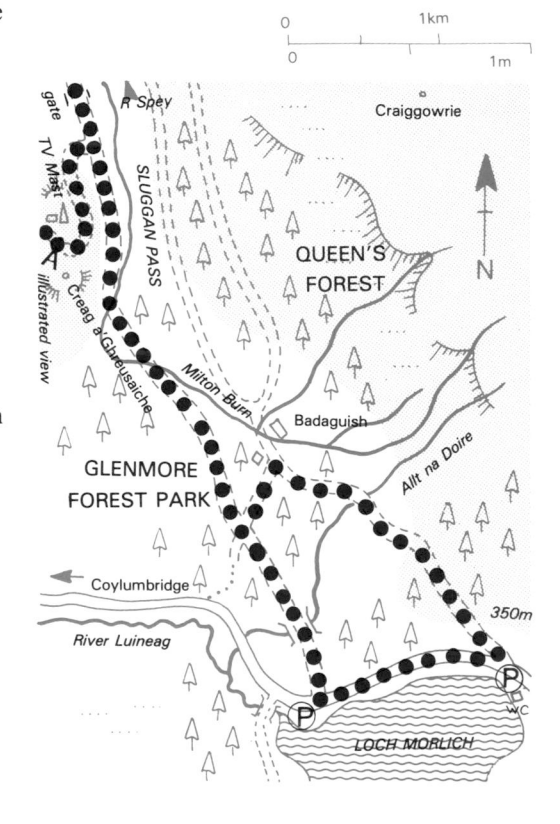

The Kincardine Hills are an arm of the Cairngorm Mountains, severed from the main body of the hills by the Ryvoan Pass *(30)*. The Sluggan (*Gullet*) is a narrow hill pass between the two most westerly peaks of the range: Creag a'Ghreusaiche (*Shoemaker's Hill*) and Craiggowrie (*Goat Hill*).

To reach this walk turn off the B970 at Coylumbridge and follow the road to Loch Morlich. The route starts at the west end of the loch.

Start walking up the path signposted to Badaguish. The early part of the way is through Scots pine forest — most of it recently planted but interspersed with relics of the original forest, some of them very large. From the end of the path, at the boundary of the Queen's Forest, there are two possible extensions. One leads to the peak of Creag a'Ghreusaiche, the other descends by the Milton Burn to the Spey Valley — a further 1½ miles (2.5km). The view from the creag is splendid (see below), if rather obscured by trees. Do not interfere with the television aerial or building at the summit.

An alternative return route is shown on the map, leading past Badaguish to Glenmore.

1. *Creag Dhubh (848m)* 2. *The Cairngorms and Loch Morlich* 3. *Ord Ban (428m)* 4. *Coylumbridge* 5. *Loch Alvie* 6. *Monadhliath Mountains* 7. *Craigellachie* 8. *Aviemore*

28 Craigellachie

Length: 2 miles (3km)
Height climbed: 250ft (80m)
Grade: C
Public conveniences: Aviemore
Public transport: Bus and train services to
Aviemore from north and south

*A short walk through natural birch wood,
with its distinctive wildlife. Paths good,
but slippery when wet.*

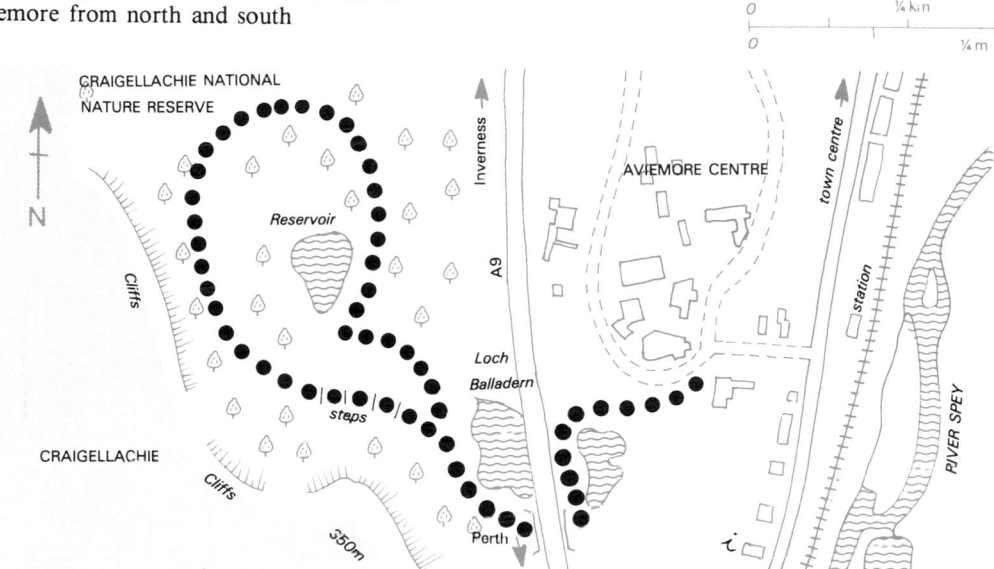

Directly behind Aviemore is Craigellachie (*The
Wutch Hill*). The name of the hill was the
caithgairm, or war cry, of the clan Grant. The
lower slopes of this hill are clothed in mature,
natural birch woodland; the upper is steep and
rocky — the nesting place of jackdaws and,
often, peregrine falcons. A section of the hill is
now a National Nature Reserve.

The start of the walk is difficult to describe,
but should be clear enough from the map. Walk
behind the lochan and cut right, under the A9.
The path is clearly marked from there on.

The way is steep in places and there are
quite a number of steps along the way, while a
good part of the route is on raised wooden
slats — these can become very slippery if it has
been raining.

The animal life in the birch wood consists
largely of the smaller mammals — mice and
voles. Bird life, apart from the peregrines,
includes a great many of the smaller species:
tits and finches, goldcrest, wren, wagtail and
siskin. A complete list is provided in a leaflet
available in Aviemore.

From the higher section of the walk there is
a fine view across Aviemore and Speyside to
the Cairngorms. The ski slopes beyond Loch
Morlich are visible on clear days.

Because of the nesting falcons visitors are
asked to stay on the paths, particularly if
walking between April and July — the nesting
period.

29 Serpent's Loch

Length: 4 miles (6.5km)
Height climbed: Negligible
Grade: B
Public conveniences: Glenmore
Public transport: Bus service between Aviemore and the ski slopes; stops at Glenmore

A level forest walk through a variety of conifer types and ages, passing Loch Morlich. Paths good.

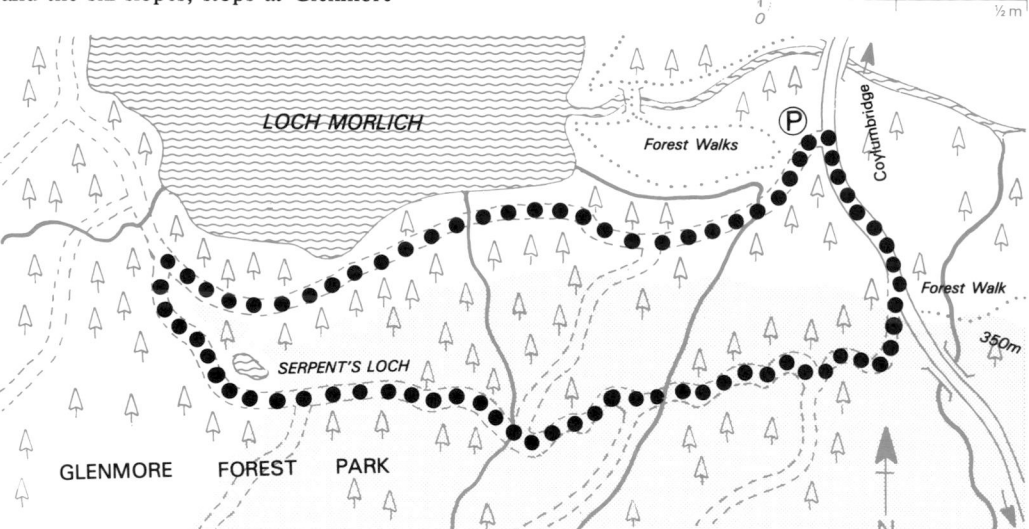

Follow the ski road from Coylumbridge to Loch Morlich. The car park is just beyond the loch on the right hand side beyond the river.

This route is one of a number of forest walks in the Glenmore Forest Park. A leaflet is available from tourist information centres giving details of the other routes in the area. For this route follow the red posts. The route is never in doubt and the conditions are very easy. At one stage the path runs along the side of Loch Morlich, giving pleasant views across the water. Unlike much of the forestry in Glenmore there is considerable variety of conifers in this part of the forest — larch, spruce and pine.

On the outward stretch of the walk the Cairngorms are visible to the left of the path, the conical peak of Carn Eilrig being prominent. On the return route the summit of Meall a'Bhuachaille (*The Shepherd's Hill*) (*30*), the most easterly of the Kincardine Hills, is visible above the trees, with Creag nan Gall (*The Stranger's Hill*) across the Ryvoan Pass to its right.

The Serpent's Loch is a tiny lochan surrounded by trees, near the turn of the walk.

30 Meall a'Bhuachaille

Length: 5 miles (8km)
Height climbed: 1550ft (470m)
Grade: A
Public conveniences: Glenmore
Public transport: Bus service from Aviemore to the ski slopes; stops at Glenmore

A splendid, steep hill climb giving tremendous views in all directions, including towards the Cairngorms. The path is rough, faint and wet in various places.

Walk 30

Turn off the B970 at Coylumbridge and take the ski road up to Glenmore. Park at the car park by the Forestry Commission office. In the car park there is a monument commemorating the Norwegian troops who were trained at Glenmore during World War II.

From the car park follow the sign pointing to the 'Shepherd's Hill Trek' (from a translation of the hill's name). This route is one of those listed in the 'Glenmore Forest Park' leaflet, and the way is marked by a series of green stakes.

The early part of the route is a gentle climb through a dense plantation of pines. To the left a burn can be heard tumbling through the forest. Here and there are small groups of the older, naturally sown Scots pine: relics of the Caledonian pine forest.

Halfway to the summit (at about 1000ft (480m) the path breaks out of the plantation, steepens and becomes very wet as it heads directly towards the saddle between Meall a'Bhuachaille and Creagan Gorm (*Blue Hill*) past scattered pine trees.

Once on the saddle the path splits. To the left it climbs to the peak of Creagan Gorm and then continues to Craiggowrie and down to the Sluggan Pass *(27)*. The other path, which this route follows, turns right, up to the summit of the meall. At the top there is a large cairn which offers some protection from the elements — often necessary — and a chance to admire the splendid views of the Cairngorms and Speyside in relative comfort.

Walk down the path on the opposite side of the hill. This is very steep in places, but the views are superb. The red tin roof of Ryvoan Bothy can be seen at the foot of the hill and beyond that, the loch-studded moorland towards Bynack and Strath Nethy. Turn right at Ryvoan. The path is very clear from this point on.

After ½ mile (1km) a path cuts off to the left: this is the Cateran's Road (*the Robber's Road*) to Loch Avon and beyond.

Ryvoan Pass, with its scree-covered slopes between clusters of Scots pine, is a romantic spot. In the days before there were roads hill passes such as this one were in constant use. Cattle were commonly driven through here: either legally, on their way to the southern fairs, or illegally, the booty from some clan raid.

At the heart of the pass is little Lochan Uaine (*Green Loch*). Oddly enough the waters *are* green, varying from a light turquoise at the water's edge to a deep bottle green.

The path continues beside Allt na Feith Duibhe (*Black Bog Burn*) back into the commercial forestry. The track becomes surfaced at Glenmore Lodge (a Scottish Sports Council training centre) and then continues, straight back to the car park.

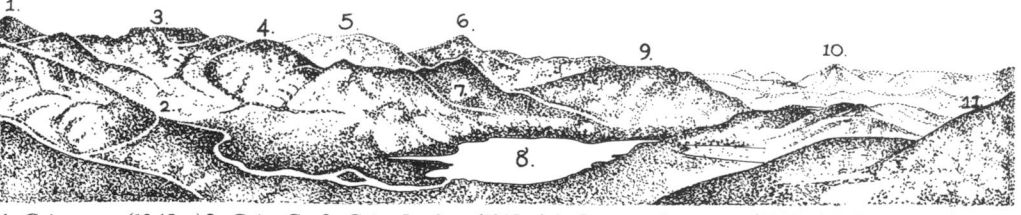

1. *Cairngorm (1245m)* 2. *Coire Cas* 3. *Cairn Lochan (1215m)* 4. *Creag na Leacainn (1053m)* 5. *Braeriach (1296m)* 6. *Sgorran Dubh Mór (1111m)* 7. *Carn Eilrig (742m)* 8. *Loch Morlich* 9. *Creagan Dhubh (848m)* 10. *Creag Dhubh (717m)* 11. *Monadhliath Mountains*

31 Cairngorm

Length: 4 miles (6.5km)
Height climbed: 2000ft (600m)
Grade: A
Public conveniences: Ski centres
Public transport: Bus service between Aviemore and the ski slopes

A steep hill climb above the ski slopes of Cairngorm. The ground is rough, and it can be cold and misty on the top. Superb views.

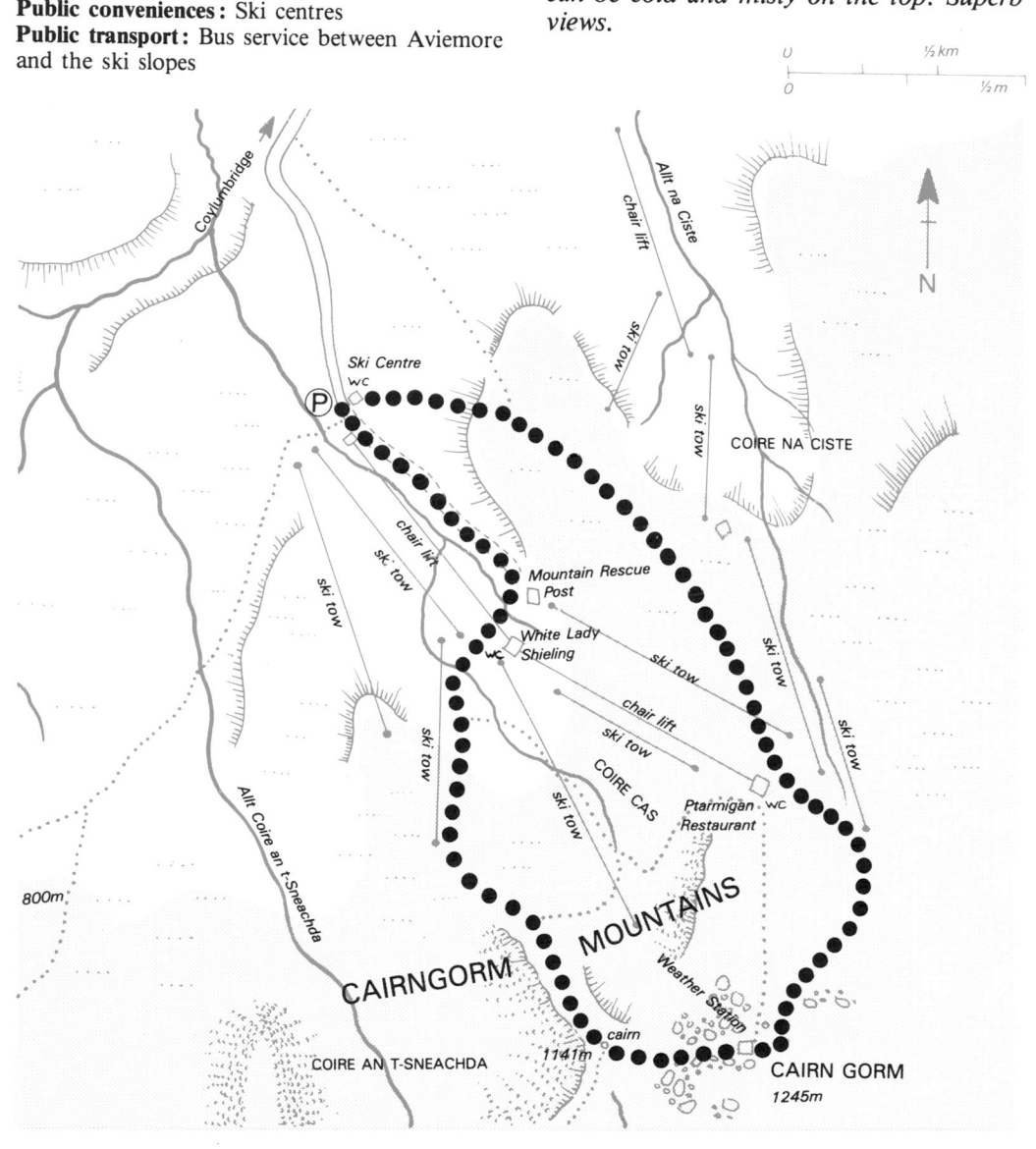

The highest peak in Scotland is Ben Nevis in Lochaber (4406ft/1342m), but the highest massif is the granite block of the Cairngorms — characterised by their rounded peaks and high plateaux intersected by deep glacial valleys. These hills include four peaks over 4000ft — Ben Macdui (4206ft/1309m), Braeriach (4248ft/1296m), Cairn Toul (4241ft/1291m) and Cairngorm (*The Blue Hill*) (4084ft/1245m). This last is the most easily accessible of the peaks, since a road was built up to its lower slopes to provide access to the ski slopes — indeed, for those who feel disinclined to climb the hill there is a chairlift to within 600ft (180m) of the summit.

To reach the walk take the road from Aviemore to Coylumbridge and then follow the ski road up to Coire Cas. There is a large car park here, and a full range of facilities in the ski centre at the foot of the chair lift. The ski slopes run down the sides of the corrie; where the glaciers of the ice age gouged a concave hollow from the side of the mountain.

There is no particular path up the mountain. Start walking up the path along the floor of the corrie, and then cut up to the left, beyond the bottom ski centre, on to the ridge of Sron an Aonaich. Follow the ridge up to the Ptarmigan Restaurant — the highest in the country — at the top of the chairlift. The going is steep but easy. The hill has a covering of pink granite chips. It was the colour of this rock which gave the mountains their original Gaelic name: Monadh Ruaidh (*The Red Mountains*). There is only sparse vegetation.

Beyond the restaurant there is a flight of steps to the summit. The surrounding landscape is one of broad, rocky, level ridges and deep corries; the views beyond are too vast and too spectacular to illustrate or describe — just be certain to choose a clear day for the climb; check the forecast and watch for low clouds which can cut visibility completely.

Walk westwards to the rocky cairn above Coire Cas and then continue down the ridge of Fiacaill a'Choire Chais to the White Lady Shieling. On this section be careful not to go too close to the corrie edge: there are steep cliffs here. Also, as the snow often lingers late into the summer on these hills, it is important not to venture on to any remaining patches — particularly near the corrie edges. The snow is unstable and often overhangs the cliffs.

Among the bird life of the tops the ptarmigan — white in winter; mottled grey in summer — is the commonest species, but the rarer dotterel and snow bunting may also be seen.

One peculiar feature of the area is its herd of reindeer. These animals disappeared from the Highlands about 1000 years ago, but were reintroduced from Lapland in the 1950's.

32 Rothiemurchus

Length: 6 miles (9.5km)
Height climbed: 600ft (180m)
Grade: B
Public conveniences: Glenmore
Public transport: Bus service between Aviemore and the ski slopes; stops at Glenmore

A long forest walk to the foot of the pass of Lairig Ghru and back, through the natural Scots pine of Rothiemurchus Forest. Paths generally good but rough and wet in places.

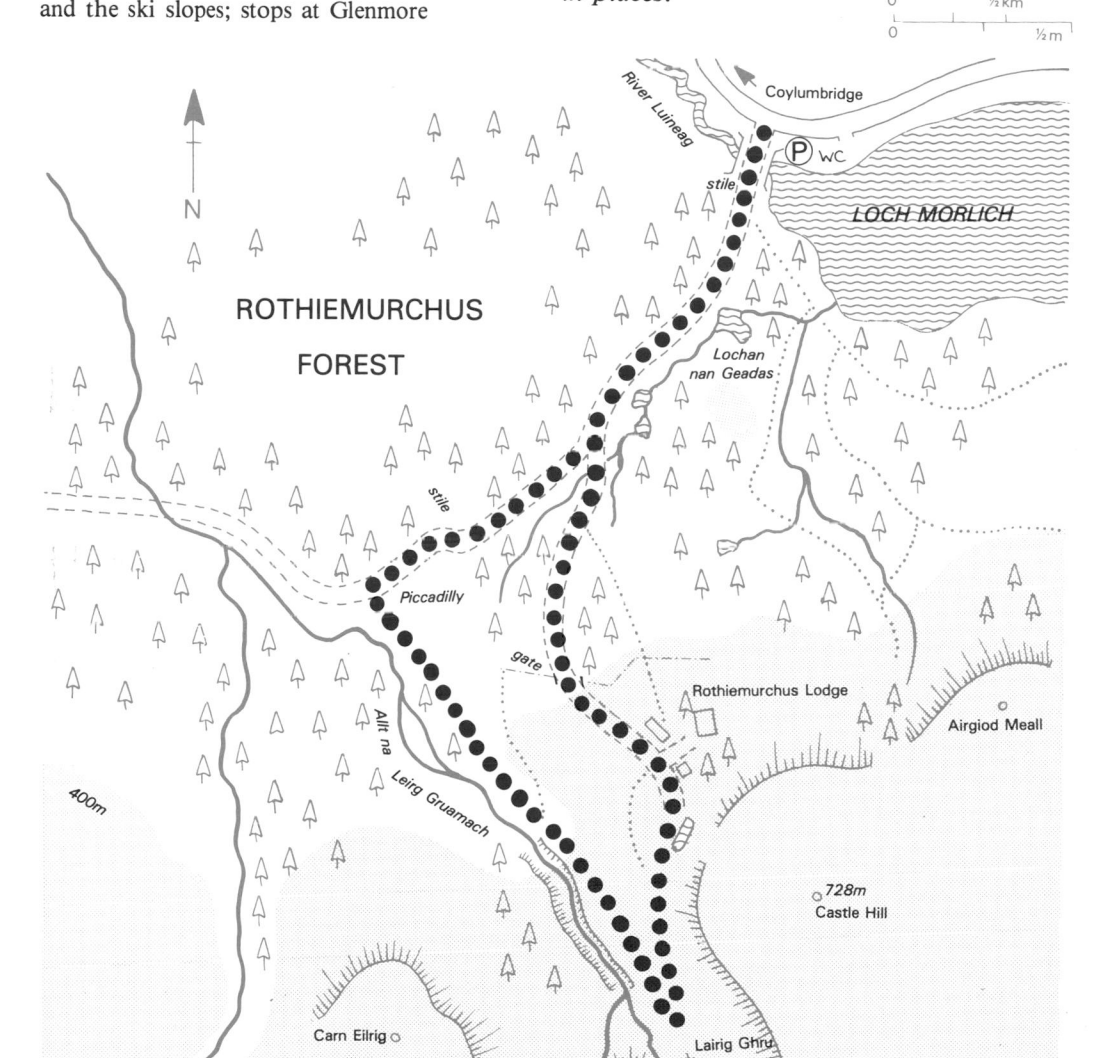

The Caledonian Pine Forest, which once covered the greater part of the Scottish Highlands, now exists only in scattered patches. This vast forest — which consisted almost entirely of the sole native conifer: the Scots pine — was reduced over the years by axe, fire and climatic changes. The latter reduced the species' ability to regenerate. Foresters took the wood for shipbuilding and firewood and, more recently, to provide ammunition boxes in the two world wars. It is their rarity, in particular, which makes these surviving fragments so interesting and important. Speyside has some of the finest remaining fragments, and this walk passes through one of them.

Leave the B970 at Coylumbridge and take the ski road to Loch Morlich. Park at the first car park by the loch side. A short distance back down the road there is a bridge which crosses the River Luineag (*The Surging River*) just as it leaves Loch Morlich.

The walk starts beside the loch and then cuts right at a fork, carrying on past Lochan nan Geadas (*Loch of the Pike*). The path is a broad forestry track at this point, passing through a plantation of commercial forestry: pine and larch. Immediately ahead, above the trees, is the neat conical peak of Carn Eilrig: the last peak between the converging valleys of Gleann Einich and the Lairig Ghru. The building on the slopes of Castle Hill, to the left of the lairig, is Rothiemurchus Lodge, which is run by the combined services — the path passes this building later in the route.

A mile from the start a junction is reached. A signpost to the right points to Piccadilly; cut left here, towards Rothiemurchus Lodge.

The natural forest starts soon afterwards. At this point the trees are old and set apart in little groups — there is very little regeneration in this part of the forest. The cover remains patchy up to the lodge. Here, to the right of the path, there is a small stone with the letters LG — Lairig Ghru. Follow the path it indicates, along the edge of a small reservoir

and on, across the hillside. The path now becomes much rougher, but it is still clear. After ½ mile (1km) the path joins with another.

The Cairngorms are criss-crossed by a number of glens and gullies, carrying footpaths through the range. The narrow, wedge-shaped gap at the head of the path is the most famous of them all. The Lairig Ghru (*The Gloomy Pass*) cuts between the highest peaks in the range — Cairn Toul, Braeriach and, the highest of them all, Ben MacDui — and carries a path through to the headwaters of the River Dee. Walk a short way up the path and get the mood of the place, but not too far — it is a long hike through the pass and needs careful planning.

Turn right at the junction of the paths and walk down the edge of the steep gorge of Allt na Leirg Gruamach. At this point the path enters a sparse forest of stunted, twisted pines. The twisting is caused by the high winds at this altitude (around 1500ft/460m) and the stunting by the poverty of the soil and the low temperatures. Some of the trees are quite old but the growing season in each year is so short that they grow only slowly. As the path continues the pines gradually become larger and more numerous, and the undergrowth thickens.

There is not a great variety of plant life in the forest: the undergrowth is largely of heather and blaeberry clustered thickly around the trunks of the pines. Such bird and animal life as exists is generally shy, but the crested tit, capercaillie or Scottish crossbill — specialists of the pine forest — may be seen; or a red squirrel or even a red deer, if the weather is cold enough. Watch also for the large hills of the wood ant.

Continue on the path to the junction at Piccadilly. Turn right here. Along the next stretch of path there is a stile, but a low gate is provided for dogs. At the next junction turn left, back along the original path to the road.

33 Loch an Eilein

Length: 3 miles (5km)
Height climbed: None
Grade: C
Public conveniences: At route
Public transport: None

A short walk on good tracks through an area of great beauty. The loch includes an island with a ruined castle, and is surrounded by a forest of Scots pine.

Loch an Eilein translates as *'Loch of the Island'*, and on the island are the ruins of a castle. The building is linked with the 14th century 'Wolf of Badenoch' — Alexander Stewart: son of King Robert II — whose destructive and unpopular viceroyalty of the Highlands necessitated the use of such impregnable strongholds. There was originally a narrow causeway to the shore, but this was submerged when the loch was dammed to store water for floating logs down to the sawmills.

To reach Loch an Eilein turn off the Aviemore to Coylumbridge road about 1 mile (1.5km) from its junction with the B9152 and follow the signs. There is a car park (with a small charge), set in a pleasant bowl, surrounded by birch and Scots pine.

The path is quite clear. Leaflets about the route are available at the car park and at a small information pavilion a short way along the route.

The path itself is part of the bewildering maze of interconnected tracks through Rothiemurchus and Glenmore *(27,29,30,32)*, and paths join the main route at various points, leading off to other parts of the forest. One diversion, at the south end of Loch an Eilein, leads round little Loch Gamhna (*Loch of the Stirks*). The main route generally stays close to the loch, passing through a forest of Scots pine.

The castle was a nesting site for ospreys until the species was hunted out of Scotland at the start of the century. It is not unlikely that one of these birds — which have recently begun nesting again in the area — will be seen fishing in the loch.

34 Lower Glen Feshie

Length: 5 miles (8km)
Height climbed: 200ft (50m)
Grade: B
Public conveniences: None
Public transport: None

A walk through a variety of woodlands in and around Glen Feshie. The path is excellent, but there are occasional damp patches.

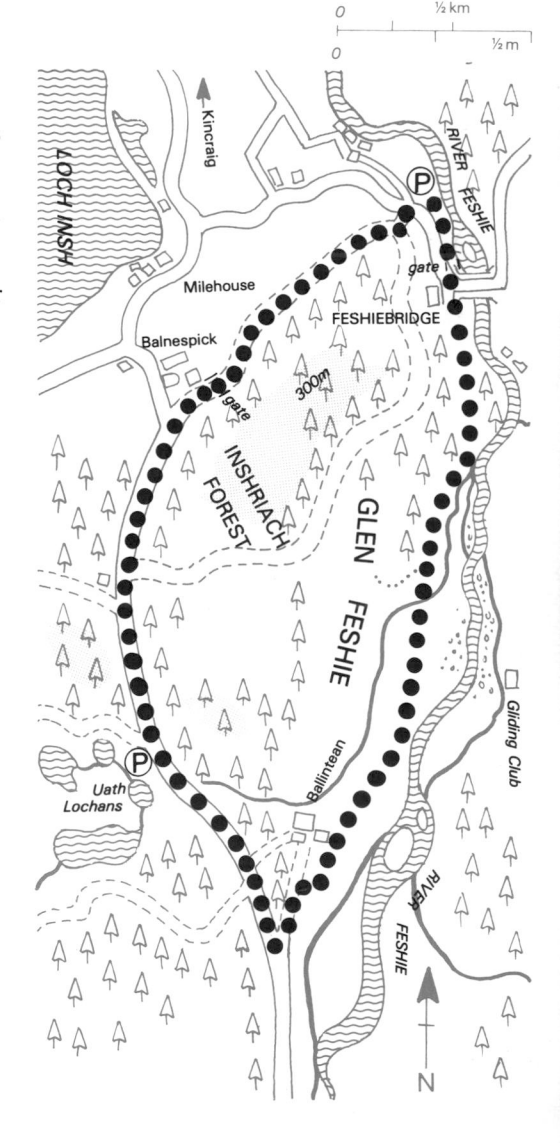

The U-shaped valley of Glen Feshie, which divides the granite mass of the Cairngorms from the lower hills of Badenoch to the east, is a typical Highland valley, formed by the erosion of the glaciers during the last ice age. The area is full of evidence of the departed ice.

To reach the start of this walk turn off the B9152 at Kincraig and turn left at the next junction. About ½ mile (1km) on there is a car park to the left of the road. A path climbs along the edge of the River Feshie and then crosses the road, just before Feshiebridge. Follow the sign to Glen Feshie and Glen Tilt.

At first the path runs beside the river, which passes through a narrow rocky defile, but it soon leaves the river and passes through a dense plantation of conifers. After leaving the plantation it drops to the flood plain of the valley, scattered with birch trees, with a long wooded ridge of glacial deposits to the right.

The way splits at one point, with the right hand path skirting round the end of the mound. Keep to the left here and cross the small burn. The path now runs close to the river, wide and shallow, meandering through the gravel deposits of the flat valley floor.

At the stables at Ballintean Farm keep to the left of the buildings and skirt up the edge of the grounds on to a path in front of a pine plantation. Follow this path on to the metalled road and turn right. Stay with this road till Balnespick; turn right here, behind the farm, and follow the path back to the road, turning right to return to the car park.

On this last stretch there are fine views of Loch Insh and the rest of the Spey Valley.

Walk 34

35 Upper Glen Feshie

Length: 8 miles (13km)
Height climbed: 200ft (60m)
Grade: A
Public conveniences: None
Public transport: None

A long walk through a variety of woodland and open moorland in a typical U-shaped Highland glen. Paths rough and wet in places.

To reach upper Glen Feshie take the road across the River Spey at Kincraig. Turn right at the junction and then left on the road sign-posted to Glen Feshie. About 3 miles (5km) along this road there is a space to park, just before the end of the public road.

Walk on along a metalled road through dense Scots pine. The plantation ends at the cottage of Stronetoper. Please pay attention to the sign here and stay off the surrounding hills between August 1 and October 20 when the stag cull is in progress. The path is quite clear now, 2 miles (3km) to the bridge at Carnachuin. Along this stretch the gradual erosion of the glacial deposits on the valley floor is clearly visible — in places the soil has been swept away by the river, revealing a deep cross-section of fine sands.

At Carnachuin there is a monument to the men who trained in the glen during the last war. It is a beautiful spot. The valley widens above the bridge and the river spreads across it in a skein of rocky channels, criss-crossing between the scattered pine on the valley floor.

On the far side of the bridge the path splits in three: the right hand fork heading for Braemar and the central path climbing in to the Cairngorms. Follow the left hand fork, returning down the glen.

The path becomes damp now as it winds through a conifer plantation. Beyond the plantation is Allt Garbhlach, flowing down from the impressive Coire Garbhlach (*Rugged Corrie*). Search for a suitable spot and jump across — this can take a little nerve when the burn is in spate.

Cross the next stretch of moorland to reach the bridge above Stronetoper and then follow the path back to the parking place.

36 Ruthven Barracks

Length: 2 miles (3km) there and back
Height climbed: None
Grade: C
Public conveniences: Kingussie
Public transport: Bus and train services to
Kingussie from north and south

*A short walk on metalled roads to the
dramatic ruins of Ruthven Barracks. A
possible moorland extension on rough
pathways.*

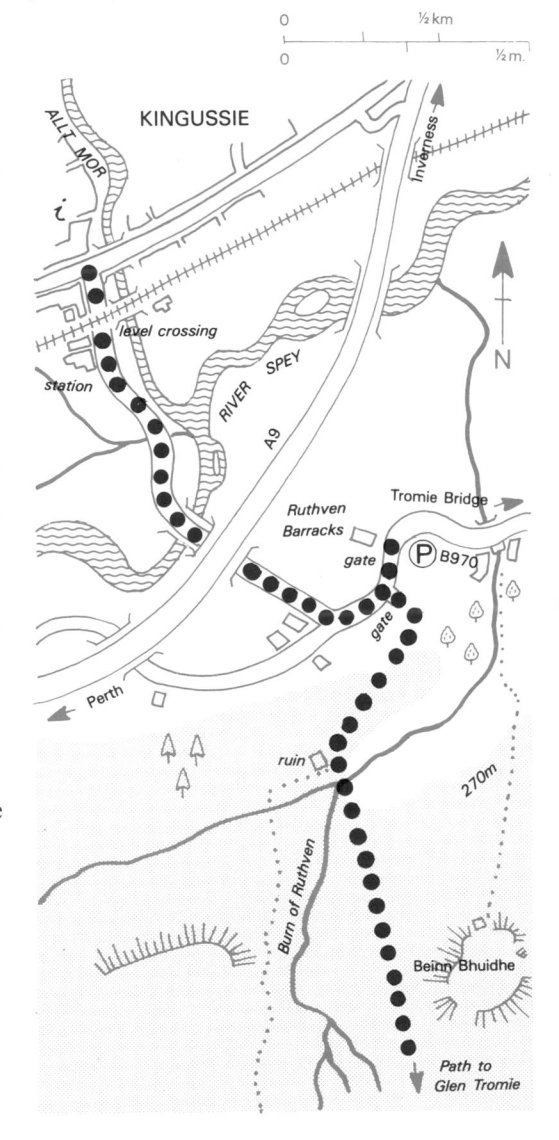

The existing building of Ruthven Barracks was
built in 1719 by the Hanoverian troops to help
control the area after the 1715 Jacobite rising,
but this splendid site had been in use for many
years before that. The first castle was built by
the Comyns in the 13th century, and a later
building was used by the infamous 'Wolf of
Badenoch'.

Start the walk at Kingussie, walking down
Ruthven road towards the station. Carry
straight on, across the level crossing. Turn left
at the junction.

The ruins sit on a grassy mound, well above
the flood plain of the River Spey — which
often does flood along this stretch of the river.
The roof has been missing since the building
was captured and burned by the Jacobite army
in 1746, but the high walls of the two main
residential blocks and the nearby stables are
still largely intact. Return by the same route.

There is a possible extension of this route —
for those wearing stout footwear — across the
moors to Glen Tromie. Fifty yards (metres)
back along the road turn left, through a gate.
The path turns sharp right, by a dyke, and
then climbs on up the hill, past a ruined
cottage, over the Ruthven Burn and on across
the moorland. Keep the peak of Beinn Bhuidhe
(*Yellow Hill*) to the left. At the top of the hill
there is a gate: turn right immediately after
this and carry on, eventually bearing left
between two hills and dropping down into the
steep-sided Glen Tromie.

It is 4 miles (6.5km) from Ruthven to Glen
Tromie. Either return by the same route or
take the road down the glen, turning left at
Tromie Bridge to return to Ruthven. This
makes a round trip of 12 miles (19km) from
Kingussie.

Walk 36

37 Creag Beg

Length: 3 miles (5km)
Height climbed: 800ft (246m)
Grade: B
Public conveniences: Kingussie
Public transport: Bus and train services to Kingussie from north and south

A brisk hill climb on rough paths. The path is occasionally steep; occasionally invisible. Tremendous views.

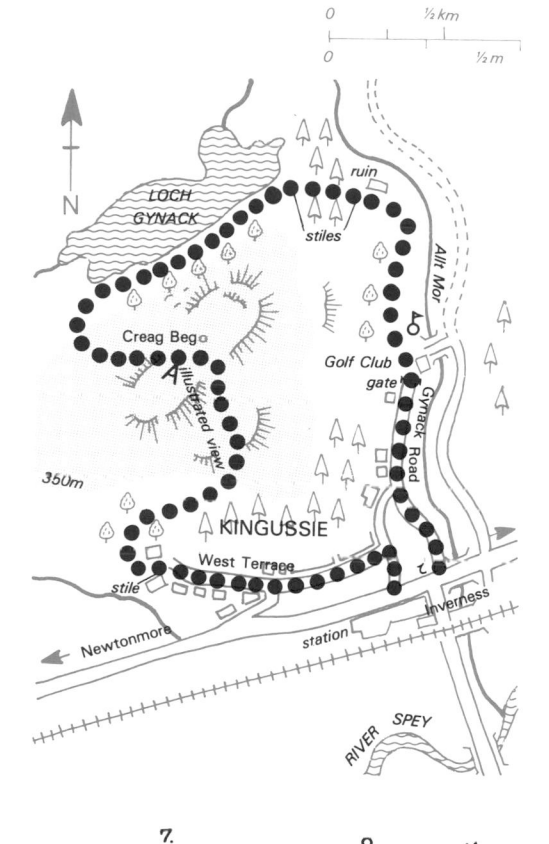

From the centre of Kingussie walk up Gynack Road, to the golf club. Walk in the main gate and cut left, up the side of the first fairway. While on the course keep an eye open for people playing, for their sakes and yours. Cut left through a thin band of woodland and skirt around the 5th green, with its ruined cottage, towards a stile across the fence.

The path is quite clear now, through a conifer plantation, across another fence and along the side of Loch Gynack. The way is rather wet here, through the scrub woodland at the base of Creag Beg.

Once out of the wood the path rises and becomes drier. Wait until the slope to the left is sufficiently shallow and start climbing: there is no particular path. The views from the top are excellent in all directions — east to the Cairngorms and Strathspey; west to Creag Dhubh above Newtonmore, Glen Banchor and the Monadhliath Mountains.

Scramble down the front of the hill, leaving the conifer plantation to the left, and wander through the birch and juniper back to Kingussie. Turn left down West Terrace to reach the town centre.

1. *Carn Dearg Mór (858m)* 2. *Cruaidhleac (640m)* 3. *Kingussie* 4. *Mullach Bheag* 5. *River Spey* 6. *Creag Bheag (491m)* 7. *Garbh Mheall Mor* 8. *Meall na Cuaich (951m)* 9. *Geal Charn (916m)* 10. *Cruba-Beag* 11. *Meall Liath (911m)* 12. *Newtonmore*

38 Green Bothy

Length: 6 miles (9.5km) there and back
Height climbed: 750ft (220m)
Grade: B
Public conveniences: Newtonmore
Public transport: Bus and train services to
Newtonmore from north and south

*A most enjoyable moorland walk, giving
fine views of the Monadhliaths and the
Hills of Badenoch. The path is very wet in
places.*

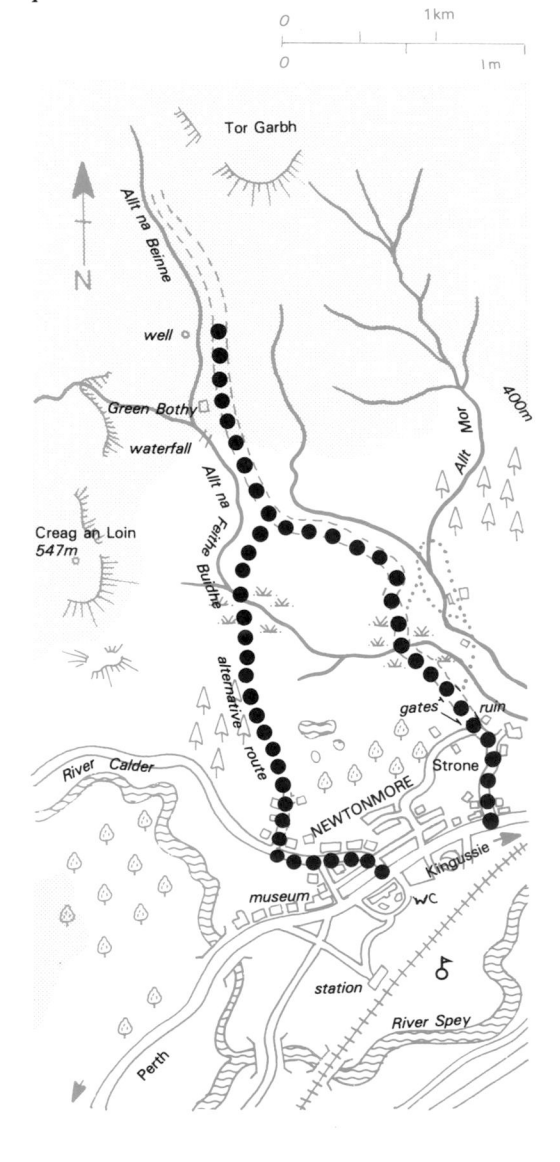

The town of Newtonmore — a small resort on
Speyside — was originally built as a clearance
village for the people who were evicted from
the surrounding hills. The area has two strong
associations: with the clan MacPherson (there
is a clan museum in the village) and with the
game of shinty — Newtonmore has produced a
number of successful teams over the years.

This route starts at the eastern end of the
village, towards Kingussie. Walk up Strone
Road. Turn right through a gate at a ruined
cottage and follow a clear path up the hill and
through a second gate. The path splits at one
point — keep left. Crossing Allt na Feithe
Buidhe (*The Burn of the Yellow Bog*) is a
potentially wet business, but it can be achieved
dry-shod by hopping from tussock to tussock.

As the path crosses the moor the hills close
in around a small glen. At the head of the glen
is a green tin hut, perched beside a waterfall.

Continue up the hill beyond the bothy for a
few minutes. There is a small cairn to the left
of the path, and a stone with the initials JD.
By the burn to the left of the path at this point
there is a spring. The soil around it has been
dyed red by the iron in the water.

Either return by the same route or turn right
at the bottom of the glen and follow the
alternative route shown on the map. This path
can be very wet.

If walking in August or later check that
there is no shooting on the hill before setting
off.

39 Dun da Lamh

Length: 4 miles (6.5km)
Height climbed: 600ft (190m)
Grade: B
Public conveniences: None
Public transport: None

A forest walk to an old hill fort, with fine views of upper Speyside and Strath Mashie. Path good, but rough near the top.

It is difficult to say how old the fort at Dun da Lamh (*Fort of the Two Hands*) is, but such a prime defensive site must surely have been utilised relatively early, and forts of this kind began to appear in Scotland around 500 BC. The tree-covered hill on which it sits rises steeply like the prow of a ship, some 600ft (180m) from the flat land at the confluence of the Spey and the Mashie.

To reach the walk take the A86 from Newtonmore, parking by a row of white houses about 1½ miles (2.5km) beyond Laggan, to the right of the road.

The route is simple. Follow the estate road over the Mashie Water and turn left at the junction. The path runs along the side of the hill through commercial forestry and then turns back, sharply, towards the summit. Where the path ends cut up to the left, along the edge of the plantation, and then approach the fort along the top of the ridge.

The view from the summit extends in every direction, including the Monadhliaths, Strathspey and the Hills of Badenoch (see below).

Return by the same route.

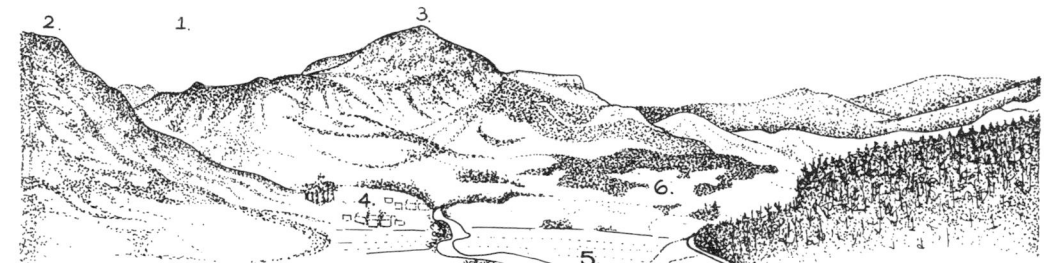

1. *The Monadhliath Mountains* 2. *Marg na Craige* 3. *Creag Dhubh (717m)* 4. *Laggan* 5. *Strathmashie* 6. *Strathspey*

40 Pattack Forest

Length: 2½ miles (4km) there and back
Height climbed: 500ft (150m)
Grade: C
Public conveniences: None
Public transport: None

A short steep walk through commercial forestry to a viewpoint above Strath Mashie.

To reach this walk take the A86 road from Newtonmore to Laggan. About 3½ miles (5.5km) beyond Laggan there is a car park to the right of the road.

On the opposite side of the road are the lower Falls of Pattack, and a short detour will provide a good view of the lowest basin. It is a romantic spot, with the water thundering into a wide, rocky pool, overhung by rowans, birch, pine and larch. This point is the watershed of Scotland: all rivers to the east of here empty into the North Sea, but the Pattack flows to the Atlantic.

Recross the road to the car park. The route is perfectly clear, wandering up the hillside through dense forestry, to the viewpoint at Black Craig. The view is extensive. West — back down the path — is Loch Laggan, which provides water for the aluminium smelter at Fort William. On a clear day Ben Nevis can be seen beyond the loch. Below is Strath Mashie while, looking down the Spey, there is a good view of the peak of Creag Dhubh above Newtonmore.

A similar but rather better view can be had from Dun da Lamh *(39)*, but the walk is longer and the climb higher.

Return by the same route.

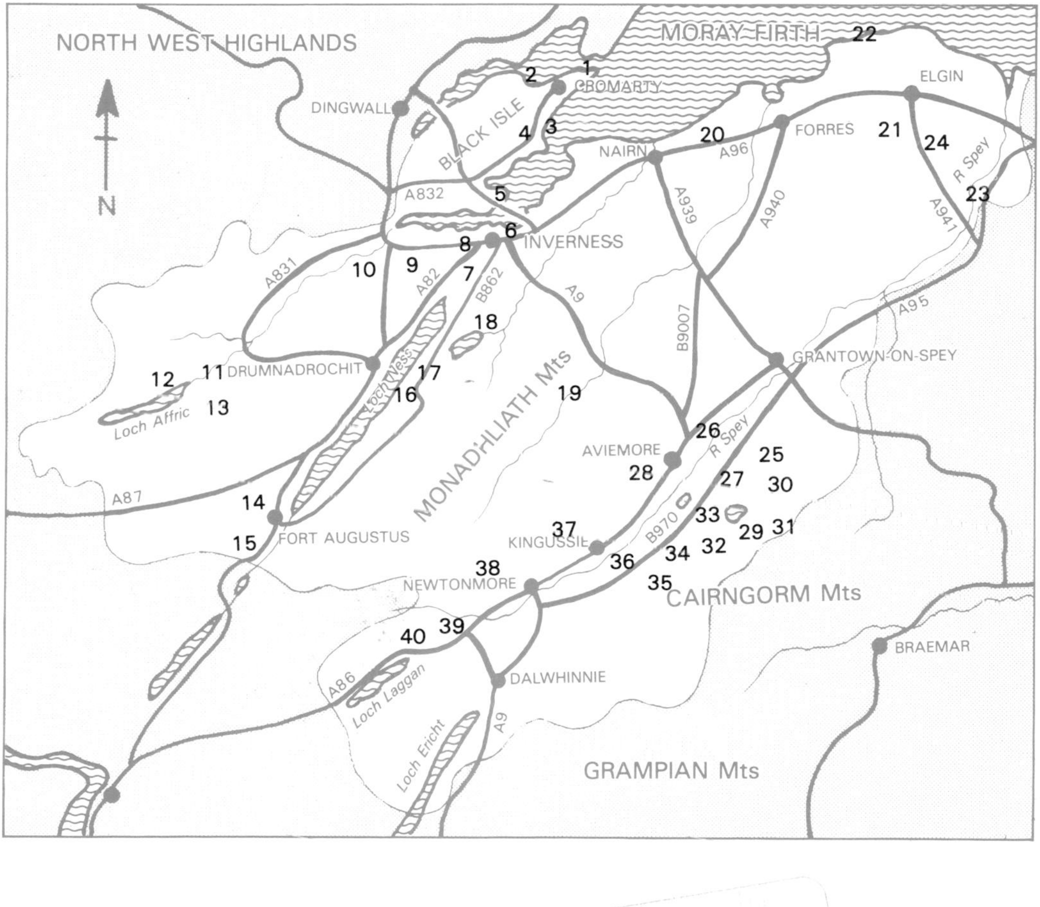

NORTH WEST HIGHLANDS

MORAY FIRTH

22

DINGWALL

ELGIN

BLACK ISLE

2 1
CROMARTY

4 3

NAIRN

20

A96

FORRES

21

24

R Spey

A832

5

A831

A939

A940

A941

23

8 6 INVERNESS

10 9 7

A82

B862

18

A9

B9007

A95

GRANTOWN-ON-SPEY

12 11 DRUMNADROCHIT

17

16

MONADHLIATH Mts

19

26

Loch Affric

13

R Spey

25

AVIEMORE

27 30

28

A87

14

B970

33

FORT AUGUSTUS

15

37

KINGUSSIE

36

29 31

34 32

38

NEWTONMORE

35

CAIRNGORM Mts

40 39

BRAEMAR

A86

Loch Laggan

DALWHINNIE

Loch Ericht

A9

GRAMPIAN Mts